Prophecy
for
TODAY

Discovery House

P U B L I S H E R S

BOX 3566 · GRAND RAPIDS, MI 49501

*PUBLISHING BOOKS THAT FEED
THE SOUL WITH THE WORD OF GOD.*

Prophecy for TODAY

God's Purpose and Plan for Our Future

J. DWIGHT PENTECOST

Prophecy for Today
First edition copyright © 1961 by Zondervan Publishing House
Copyright renewed © 1989 by J. Dwight Pentecost
Revised edition copyright © 1989 by J. Dwight Pentecost

The last three chapters of this book are taken from *Will Man Survive?*
by J. Dwight Pentecost, copyright © 1971 by The Moody Bible Institute

Discovery House Publishers is affiliated with RBC Ministries, Grand
Rapids, Michigan 49512

Unless indicated otherwise, all Scripture quotations are from the *King
James Version*

ISBN 0-929239-11-3

Printed in the United States of America

98 99 00 01 02 / CHG / 20 19 18 17 16 15 14 13 12 11 10 9

To my parents
who early guided me to a knowledge of Him,
whom to know aright is life eternal

Contents

Preface

There is a great difference between prophesying and studying prophecy. Those who attempt to prophesy and see the fulfillment of prophecy in current events will continually be forced to revise their interpretations. But those who study what the Word teaches will find that their interpretations stand the test of time.

In presenting this second edition of a book that has been in circulation for years I have not had to change the interpretations of Scripture originally given. What I presented then has stood the test of time. The truth of the Word does not change, but our understanding of it may be enlarged.

In reissuing this work I desire that our comprehension of the truths of God's Word will be enlarged and that our hope in the imminent coming of Christ will be heightened so that we all will join with John in praying, "Even so come, Lord Jesus."

Preface to First Edition

"Blessed be the God and Father of our Lord Jesus Christ, who according to his great mercy begat us again unto a *living hope* by the resurrection of Jesus Christ from the dead, unto an inheritance incorruptible, and undefiled, and that fadeth not away, reserved in heaven for you, who by the power of God are guarded through faith unto a salvation ready to be revealed in the last time" (1 Peter 1:3–5 ASV).

We live in momentous days. Events of great significance appear on the horizon, causing God's children to expect at any moment the Lord Jesus Christ, who will lift us from this earth into the presence of His glory. Our attention turns to the prophetic Scriptures to find light in this present darkness. We have a widespread hunger to know the truths of God's prophetic Word.

A number of years ago I delivered a series of messages on the major themes of prophecy to the congregation of Grace Bible Church of Dallas, Texas. Many who heard those messages encouraged me to put them into a book, which I did. This is the result.

These chapters present in a non-technical fashion some of the great themes of prophecy so that laypeople can trace these subjects through the Scriptures. Those who want to study the truths more thoroughly should consult *Things to Come*, my study of biblical eschatology. Although this presentation is popular and cursory, I have tried to give a satisfying survey of the subject.

I express my deep appreciation to Mrs. Paul Allen, Mrs. Jack Arnold, and Mrs. Offie Bayless for their contribution in transcribing the messages from tapes and in typing the manuscript. Without their assistance I could not have prepared this book.

May the Lord of glory, who has called us unto His heavenly glory, bring us the joy and confidence that comes from understanding the fullness of our "living hope."

1

Why Study Prophecy?

John 14:1–6

MANY PEOPLE TODAY relegate the prophetic Scriptures to oblivion. What we have here and now, they say, is far more important than what will happen in the future. This is particularly true among those who have no respect for the authority and integrity of God's Word. Since they do not believe that God gave us the Word, they do not believe He revealed the future in it.

Yet the prophetic Scriptures occupy a great portion of the Bible. In both the Old and New Testaments, whole books are devoted to the subject. In fact, approximately one-fourth of the Bible was prophetic when it was written. If God devoted that much space to the subject, certainly we should pay attention to it.

There are, however, some dangers in the study of prophecy. When Paul came into Athens, which controlled so much of the cultural, intellectual, and social life of Greece, he found that "all the Athenians and strangers which were there spent their time in nothing else, but either to tell, or to hear some new thing" (Acts 17:21). Athenian culture and civilization have died out, but Athenianism never has; there are still people who delight to hear "some new thing." Therein lies the first great danger in the study of prophecy. Many have become spiritually proud because they have been taught prophetic truths. Because they are able to distinguish the king of the north from the king of the south, or differentiate between the first and second beasts, or are able to interpret Daniel's image, they think they have reached a higher spiritual plane.

At the end of two years of ministry, a young man made a startling remark to me. "I wish the men in my church had never heard of prophecy," he said.

Somewhat taken back, I replied, "Why do you say that?"

"Because the members of my board will not listen to me preach. They are confident they know far more about the Scriptures than I do. They have attended so many prophetic conferences they consider themselves authorities in the Word. Every time we come to a board meeting, it is turned into an oral examination of the preacher to see how much he knows of the details of prophecy."

Instead of supporting their pastor, these men made his life so miserable he had to move to another church. They had misused prophecy by allowing their understanding of it to produce in them a sense of pride. If our study produces pride, we have failed to use it as an instrument of the Spirit of God, whose ministry it is to reproduce the mind of Christ in us.

Another danger in the study of prophecy is that it sometimes becomes a test of fellowship. Some people are unwilling to fellowship with people who interpret prophecy differently. Instead of acknowledging Christ's position as head, they elevate prophecy to the preeminent position. Whenever we put any doctrine above Christ, we are setting up a false test of fellowship and cannot know the blessing of God. Fellowship between believers is based on the person and work of Jesus Christ in our lives, not on any doctrine or interpretation of Scripture.

Some people study prophecy so intently they completely miss the Lord Jesus Christ. Scripture was given to reveal Him. He is the Center around which all Scripture revolves. If we become so interested in the Antichrist that Christ loses the central place in our lives, and if we study the Word of God only to learn how the Beast parts his hair, and miss the Lord, we have been sidetracked from that which is preeminent. It is the Spirit's work to reveal Christ, not Antichrist, to us.

God's prophecies in Scripture have a purpose, but it isn't to satisfy our curiosity. All of us were born with a desire to know what is going to happen tomorrow. That is why fortunetellers and astrologers do such a thriving business. But God's reasons for giving us prophecy reach much higher than daily events and far beyond our earthly lives.

First, prophecy proves the authority of the Bible. The Bible is different from every other religious book in that none of the others include prophecy. The foundational books of many religions and cults interpret the past and present, but they are entirely silent about the future. The Bible, on the other hand, from its opening chapters to the end, is filled with prophetic passages.

The test of prophecy is always in its fulfillment. If that which was prophesied happens, we know that the prophecy was divinely inspired. There is no greater proof of the inspiration, validity, and authority of the Bible than that of fulfilled prophecy.

The Bible's record for reliability verifies its trustworthiness. For instance, hundreds of years before Christ was born, the Old Testament told us the time of His birth (Dan. 9); the fact of the virgin birth (Isa. 7); the place of His birth (Mic. 5); the intimate details of His life and death (Ps. 22 and Isa. 53); and the fact of His resurrection (Ps. 16).

One mathematician calculated the probability of all the prophecies concerning the first coming of Christ coming true. He determined that there was only one chance in 87 plus 93 zeros that the Bible could be right on the basis of guess alone.

God has revealed and fulfilled some prophecies to prove that Scripture is of divine origin, trustworthy, and to be studied with confidence. After all, everything we know about God comes from His Word. If it is not trustworthy, we have no revelation at all. But fulfilled prophecy proves to us that God knows the future, and a God who knows the future is a God who can be trusted.

Second, prophecy reveals God's power and wisdom. When we understand the prophetic Scriptures, we come to a deeper knowledge of the power and wisdom of God. For instance, prophecy was given through Isaiah to reveal God's power and wisdom to King Ahaz and the nation Israel.

Ahaz, known for his godlessness, descended to new depths of degradation when he led the children of Israel into gross forms of idolatry. In spite of this God sent Isaiah to Ahaz to announce that God would defend His people from a threatened invasion and certify His word with a sign—any sign Ahaz might request. "Ask thee a sign of the Lord thy God; ask it either in the depth, or in the height above" (Isa. 7:11). Ahaz could have asked God to bring someone back from the dead or to turn the sun backward in its course, as God had done in the days of Ahaz's forebears. This sign was to bring Ahaz to repentance. But Ahaz replied, "I will not tempt the Lord." This was not humility on the king's part; Ahaz was forbidding God to intervene in the affairs of the nation Israel. Although God said He would punish the nation for their iniquity, Ahaz thought he could prevent it by not choosing a sign. By denying God an opportunity to show His sign, Ahaz thought he could remove his obligation to submit to God.

Isaiah responded by saying, "The Lord himself shall give you a sign; Behold, a virgin shall conceive, and bear a son, and shall call his name Immanuel." Through Isaiah, God prophesied Christ's virgin birth more than 700 years before the actual event (Isa. 7). To understand this prophecy more fully, we have to realize that there were two sons in view here. One was Isaiah's son, referred to in verse 3, "Go now and meet Ahaz, thou, and Shearjashub thy son." Isaiah took his son, perhaps still a child, with him for the encounter with Ahaz. He is the first son. Isaiah told Ahaz that before the son in his arms grows big enough to know the difference between good and evil, the people will be scattered. Because Ahaz refused to repent, God was revealing an imminent judgment, which Ahaz himself would witness. This led to the mention of the second son, the virgin-born Son, who, some 750 years in the future, would come to bring judgment on the nation that rejected Him. God revealed to Ahaz both the near and distant future to show that He is a God of wisdom and power, and that no wicked, godless king can prevent Him from doing what He has purposed to do.

Third, prophecy reveals the purposes of God. In Genesis 18, God appeared to Abraham and revealed His purpose by telling him that the wicked cities of Sodom and Gomorrah were going to be destroyed. "The Lord said, Shall I hide from Abraham that thing which I do; seeing that Abraham shall surely become a great and mighty nation, and all the nations of the earth shall be blessed in him?" (Gen. 18:17).

God took Abraham into intimate fellowship and revealed what He purposed to do. Abraham would live to see the destruction of those cities. Without this revelation, Abraham might well have asked, "Why did God do that? What was the purpose of destroying all that human life?" God revealed His plan and purpose to Abraham so he would understand that God was holy and could no longer tolerate the sin of the people.

God revealed this prophecy to Abraham so he would understand the purpose of God, and through the study of the prophetic Scriptures we can understand the unfolding purpose of God today.

As we study some of the great events in prophecy we will see that God revealed His plans and purposes to us so that our hearts shall not give way to fear when it appears as though God has been deposed from His throne and the world has gotten out of His control. Nothing will assure us that God is working all things according to the counsel of His own will as much as knowing that all things are moving according to His predetermined and prophesied program. Prophecy will bring us into an intimate knowledge of the purpose of God.

Fourth, prophecy brings peace to believers. The Lord Jesus said, "Let not your heart be troubled, Ye believe in God, believe also in me" (John 14:1). He had just told His disciples He was going to leave them. He had predicted His death and resurrection. Up to this point, the disciples had been under His tutelage; they had been provided for by His power; they had been guided by His Word. Their whole life had centered on Him. Now He tells them He is going away. What will they do? Who will provide for them, guide them, teach them, and protect them from their enemies? Christ gave them assurance by revealing a prophetic event, "In my Father's house are many mansions: if it were not so, I would have told you. I go to prepare a place for you. And if I go and prepare a place for you, I will come again, and receive you unto myself; that where I am, there ye may be also" (John 14:2–4). The answer to their heart trouble was faith; faith in the person of God ("ye believe in God, believe also in me") and faith in the program of God ("in my Father's house are many mansions" and "I will come again and receive you unto myself"). The purpose of Christ's prophecy to His disciples was to give them peace, and peace is one of the great results of studying prophecy.

We can hardly pick up a newsmagazine or watch the evening news without hearing about war somewhere in the world. Yet the child of God who is acquainted with the prophetic Scriptures rests in assurance because we have God's own blueprint of His plans for this world and its civilizations. When night draws dark around us, God's Sun of Righteousness will guide us.

Fifth, God's great purpose in prophecy is to produce in His children a holy life. A study of prophecy that does not result in holy living has not fulfilled its purpose.

A short time ago, I noted each reference in the New Testament to the coming of Christ and asked myself what it taught. Almost without exception, New Testament references to the coming of Christ are followed by an exhortation to godliness and holy living.

Although the study of prophecy will give us proof of the authority of the Word of God, will reveal the purpose and power of God, and will give us the peace and assurance of God, we have missed the whole purpose if it does not conform us to the image of God.

In Philippians 3 Paul expressed the great desire of his heart—to know Christ and to be conformed to Him. He wrote, "Not as though I had already attained, either were already perfect: but I follow after, if that I may apprehend [lay hold of] that for which also I am apprehended [have been laid hold of] by Christ Jesus. Brethren, I count not myself to have apprehended [laid hold]: but this one thing I do, forgetting those things which are behind, and reaching forth unto those things which are before, I press toward the mark for the prize of the high calling of God in Christ Jesus" (Phil. 3:12–14). In this statement Paul revealed that he lived his whole life in view of the coming of Christ. In verse 20 he wrote, "Our conversation is in heaven" or, as it may be rendered, "the state of which we are citizens is heaven," and then adds, "from whence also we look for the Saviour, the Lord Jesus Christ: who shall change our vile body, that it may be fashioned like unto his glorious body, according to the working whereby he is able even to subdue all things unto himself." Paul viewed himself as an absentee citizen. In Philippians 4:1 he con-

cluded this teaching with an affirmation of Christ's coming. In view of that event, they were to stand fast in the
Lord.

In Colossians 3:1–3, he gave us the assurance of our
identification with Christ. In verse 4 he wrote, "When
Christ, who is our life, shall appear, then shall ye also
appear with him in glory." We are to "put off" the sins of
the flesh (v. 5) and "put on" the manifestations of the
Spirit (v. 12).

In Titus 2:11, Paul reminded his readers of the grace of
God, which includes the precious expectation of Christ's
return (v. 13). In verse 12 he exhorted them to deny
"ungodliness and worldly lusts" and to live "soberly, righ-
teously, and godly in this present world" while anticipating the second coming of Christ.

Finally, in 2 Peter 3, where Peter outlined the prophetic
events, he said, "The day of the Lord will come as a thief
in the night; in the which the heavens shall pass away with
a great noise, and the elements shall melt with fervent
heat, the earth also and the works that are therein shall be
burned up" (v. 10). In verse 11 he gave the application:
"Seeing then that all these things shall be dissolved, what
manner of persons ought ye to be in all holy manner of life
and godliness, looking for and hasting unto the coming of
the day of God. . . . Wherefore, beloved, seeing that ye
look for such things, be diligent that ye may be found of
him in peace, without spot, and blameless." Peter has
added his testimony to Paul's that the study of prophecy
must produce a holy life.

When asked to visit a certain home, I promised I would
be there at my first opportunity. Several days later I found
time to stop by the family's house. They welcomed me

most cordially and invited me into the living room. During the visit, several small children came into the room and looked first at me and then at their parents. Then they slipped away with the comment, "Good, he's come. Now home can be home again." The mother smiled and explained. In anticipation of my visit the living room had been all tidied up and the children were not permitted to play there until after the pastor called, lest it be untidy when he arrived. The anticipation of a stranger's visit had produced a different kind of life in that home!

Likewise, Christ has told us He will come. Only the time is uncertain. May the joy of looking for Him produce in us a holy life so that we will not be ashamed when we see Him.

2

The Next Event in the Prophetic Program

1 Thessalonians 4:13–18

WHAT IS THE NEXT EVENT in God's prophetic program? Some expect the tribulation; some anticipate Armageddon; and some look for the Beast and the False Prophet. Had any of those been the apostle Paul's highest expectation he hardly could have written about "the blessed hope and the glorious appearing of the great God and our Saviour, Jesus Christ." The thought of living through the conflagration of Armageddon gives joy to no one, nor is it pleasant to anticipate life under the iron fist of the Beast.

That next event for the believer is the translation or rapture of the church. When God is ready to terminate this age, the Lord Jesus Christ will appear in the air to take all believers to Himself.

Shortly before His crucifixion, Jesus took His disciples to an upper room to prepare them for His absence (John 13). He explained what had happened during their years together and revealed to them what would soon take place. In verse 21 He announced His betrayal and in verse 31 He announced His death, causing Peter to ask, "Lord, whither goest thou?" To this Jesus replied, "Whither I go, thou canst not follow me now; but thou shalt follow me afterwards." This discourse revealed that not only was Christ going to die, but that He was going to be separated from the disciples as well. They would no longer see Him or walk with Him. This shocking revelation gave the disciples a severe spiritual heart attack. Responding to their need, the Lord Jesus said, "Let not your heart be troubled."

They had every reason to be disturbed. The One who had been their closest friend would no longer be with them. The One who had provided for them would no longer be present to meet their needs. The One who had been their guide would no longer be around to give them direction. The One who had empowered them would no longer be available to give them strength. They would be left as orphans, as children without a father.

The Lord met this spiritual problem in two ways. First, He issued a call to faith: "Ye believe in God, believe also in me." He called them to faith in God the Father and faith in God the Son. Second, He delivered a promise that called for faith in His program: "In my Father's house are many mansions [or dwelling-places, or apartments]: if it were not so, I would have told you. I go to prepare a place for you, I will come again, and receive you unto myself; that where I am there ye may be also." After talking to them about His death and separation from them, He pointed ahead to a time when the absent One would again be present; when the orphaned ones will have a Father;

when those who have been separated from the Father will be brought into His very presence.

The deep need of the disciples was met by a promise: "And if I go and prepare a place for you [and I most certainly will], I will come again, and receive you unto myself; that where I am there ye may be also." The word translated *prepare* does not mean to make or manufacture. It means, as some of our Southern friends would say, "to ready up, to furnish or to equip, to make it into a suitable habitation for the one who is to be moved into this place." The Lord Jesus is pictured, not as creating a new dwelling place, but as taking an existing habitation and preparing, furnishing, and equipping it for those He will receive to Himself at His coming.

The Lord had an Oriental dwelling in mind when He used this symbol to teach the disciples about their future abode. In the society in which Christ lived, the houses were built around a large open patio. Normally the outside walls had no openings, with the exception of a large main door or gate that opened into the patio and could be barred for protection. Upon entering this gate or door, a person would see a number of rooms that opened onto the central square. When a father found a bride for his son, he would go to an unused portion of the enclosure and wall off another room or two. This addition would become the habitation of the son and his bride. As the family increased, walls would be added and the living quarters expanded. When we read, "In my Father's house are many mansions," it usually brings to mind a beautiful, earthly edifice, polished and adorned with gold or silver, translated into glory. But that is not the picture the Lord has in view at all. Rather He is saying that in the enclosure called the Father's house, there will be many apartments, or dwelling places. This emphasizes the unity of the family—we will be united one with another and with the Father.

The Lord's promise that He is preparing a place for us includes another promise: "I will come again, and receive you unto myself; that where I am, there ye may be also." As it is natural for the bridegroom to keep the bride with him wherever he goes, our Lord, because of His love for us, wants to be with us. He is preparing a dwelling place for us as a bridegroom does for a bride, that we might be in His presence, at home with Him forever.

In John 14, Christ told us only that He is coming again to take us to Himself. Of the program, the method, and the time, He said nothing. To get further instruction about this great program of the translation of the church, we must turn to 1 Corinthians 15. At the outset of his teaching about resurrection, Paul gave the two great facts of the Gospel: the death of Christ and the resurrection of Christ. "Christ died for our sins according to the scriptures" is the foundational fact, and this fact is proved, according to verse 4, by the fact that He was buried. "He rose again the third day according to the scriptures" is the supporting fact, and is proved, according to verse 5, by virtue of the fact that He was seen of Cephas, of the twelve, and then of more than 500 brethren.

A great portion of this chapter is devoted to an unfolding of the second fact of the Gospel, the resurrection of Christ. If Jesus Christ died for us but does not live again by resurrection, we do not have salvation at all. Our salvation depends not only on the death of Christ but just as much on His resurrection. So Paul moves to defend and

prove the resurrection. The resurrection of Christ demands the resurrection of all those who belong to Him. So
Paul demonstrated not only that Christ has been raised,
but that we believers will be raised also. Indeed, every
individual who ever lives will be resurrected. Some will be
resurrected to life and some to judgment. This is a serious
and sobering thought. If the unsaved and the wicked were
left in the grave forever and were never resurrected, if they
lapsed into unconsciousness never to be awakened, if they
were blotted out and forgotten, that would be the end of
them and it would not matter what they did about Christ.
They would miss the blessing and glory of heaven, but
they wouldn't be suffering. The apostle, however, revealed
that every individual will be resurrected.

After presenting the truth about resurrection, the apostle concluded his discussion by introducing what he called
"a mystery." He wrote, "I shew you a mystery; we shall not
all sleep, but we shall all be changed, in a moment, in the
twinkling of an eye, at the last trump: for the trumpet shall
sound, and the dead shall be raised incorruptible, and we
[the living ones] shall be changed" (v. 51). When the word
mystery is used in the Word of God, it does not refer to
something mysterious or difficult to understand. Rather it
refers to some truth not previously revealed by God that
we would not and could not know apart from divine
revelation.

The Old Testament had already taught the truth of the
resurrection of the body. For instance, Job said, "I know
that my redeemer liveth, and that he shall stand in the
latter day upon the earth: And though after my skin
worms destroy this body, yet in my flesh shall I see God"
(Job 19:25). Job had the confident hope of the resurrection

through the Redeemer who would one day appear. Isaiah
was possessed of the same hope. He wrote, "Thy dead
men shall live, together with my dead body shall they
arise. Awake and sing, ye that dwell in dust: for thy dew is
as the dew of herbs, and the earth shall cast out the dead"
(Isa. 26:19). Daniel held the same hope. "And many of
them that sleep in the dust of the earth shall awake, some
to everlasting life, and some to shame and everlasting
contempt" (Dan. 12:2). Christ taught the same truth when
He said, "Marvel not at this: for the hour is coming, in the
which all that are in the graves shall hear his voice, and
shall come forth; they that have done good, unto the
resurrection of life; and they that have done evil, unto the
resurrection of damnation" (John 5:28–29).

These passages show us that the righteous will be resurrected into glory and will enjoy the presence of God forever, while the wicked will be raised to judgment and
separation from God. It was not resurrection, then, that
was the mystery.

What then was the mystery? It was that some believers
would be translated into God's presence without experiencing death and resurrection.

Reading from Genesis 1 through 1 Corinthians 15, we
conclude that there is only one way to get into glory—
through physical death and physical resurrection. Except
for Enoch and Elijah, who were both translated without
seeing death, there is no hint in the Old Testament that
any other people could hope to come into God's presence
apart from death and resurrection. This is not revealed in
Scripture until we come to 1 Corinthians 15.

God knew all along that there would be a day when all
believers, like Enoch, would be "caught up," but He did

not take people into His confidence and reveal His purpose to them. When Elijah was translated and the double
portion of God's spirit fell on Elisha, even Elisha had no
idea that God one day would "catch up" every believer as
he had Elijah. That was a purpose of God, hidden away in
the recesses of His own counsels.

Through the apostle Paul God finally revealed that "we
shall not all sleep." In speaking of sleep, Paul was referring
to the believer's death. He was saying, "I want to teach you
a truth that never has been taught or revealed before. We
believers shall not all come into glory by the process of
death and resurrection. Even though entrance into glory
necessitates a change for all, this change can be accomplished without physical death, for God can change living
believers instantaneously." This then is the new truth:
there could be a transformation into the presence of
God—out of this body of corruption into an incorruptible
body, out of this mortal body into an immortal body—
without the process of death and resurrection. One whole
generation of believers one day will experience this kind of
change.

Paul then proceeded to tell how this will happen. The
first thing we observe is that it will be an instantaneous
change; it will take place "in the twinkling of an eye." A
twinkling is like the sudden flash that passes between two
individuals—that instantaneous, indivisible unit of time
in which there is a flash of recognition without any lapse
of time. Our translation is going to be that rapid. One
moment we will be on the earth, and in a twinkling we will
find ourselves in glory.

Further, Paul says that it will take place at the last
trump, which refers to that moment of time when God

will conclude this present age, when the last member of the Body of Christ is born again and joined to the Body of Christ by the baptism of the Holy Spirit. It will happen at the moment the bride of Christ is completed, when the Father will say to Christ, "Son, it is time for You to return and bring to Yourself the bride I have given You, who has been redeemed through Your blood." There is not the faintest hint any place in the Bible as to when that time will be.

Again, the apostle says, "We shall be changed." This body of corruption shall be changed into an incorruptible body and this mortal body, subject to death, shall become deathless as it is translated at that moment of time into the very presence of God and is glorified. Paul has built upon the foundation which the Lord laid in John 14 when He promised, "I will come again, and receive you unto my-self." And now Paul has told us in 1 Corinthians 15 a little bit of what that program will be as believers are caught up to meet the Lord in the air and are translated into glory.

Now let us consider 1 Thessalonians 4:13–18, where the apostle gives more detail concerning this translation, or rapture, of the church. Paul was writing to solve a problem that had come up in the Thessalonian assembly. Even though these believers were spiritual babes, Paul had not kept from them the truth about the Lord's return. Therefore, they had been living each day in the expectation of Christ's imminent return. Then a strange thing happened—some of the members of the assembly died unexpectedly. Those who survived became concerned; they were afraid that those who had died would miss the benefits of the rapture or have an inferior place in glory. They thought living believers would have the advantage at the translation. If two different groups were going to be with the Lord—one by translation and one by resurrection—they also may have concluded that there would be divisions for all eternity. And perhaps they thought that those who were alive and were translated would go to a different place than those who had been resurrected. It raised the question as to whether the living ones, who expected to be translated, would ever again see their loved ones, who would meet the Lord by resurrection.

They had not grasped the teaching of John 14, for there the Lord Jesus told the disciples that all believers would be in the "Father's house." Thus Paul needed to write to them concerning the relation of the living and the dead saints at the coming of Christ for His own.

Paul began by writing, "I would not have you to be ignorant, brethren . . ." (v. 13). When Paul said he didn't want them to be ignorant, it meant they were ignorant but he didn't want them to continue that way. Thus he was writing to dispel their ignorance. What a blessing he wrote, "For if we believe that Jesus died and rose again [and we certainly do believe that], even so them also which sleep in Jesus God will bring with him." This is the first point of his comforting consolation: Not a single believer will be left in the grave when the Lord Jesus Christ comes. We sing, "Death cannot keep his prey." Why? Because Jesus Christ is the victor over death. If, at the coming of Christ and the resurrection of believers, the body of one single believer were left behind, Satan would have won a victory. So Paul was explaining that all who have died as believers, God must bring to Himself by resurrection.

Verses 15–17 reveal the process by which the church will meet the Lord in the air. "For this we say unto you by the word of the Lord, that we which are alive and remain unto the coming of the Lord shall not prevent [precede, have a head start on] them which are asleep." It would seem as though the living ones would have a little head start on those who must come from the graves. But the apostle says that when we go to meet the Lord, the living ones will have no advantage. The reason follows: "For the Lord himself will descend from heaven with a shout, with the voice of the archangel, and with the trump of God: and the dead in Christ shall rise first: Then we which are alive and remain shall be caught up together with them in the clouds, to meet the Lord in the air: and so shall we ever be with the Lord."

Notice those three phrases: a shout, the voice of the archangel, the trump of God. The word translated "shout" here was used as a military command similar to "Forward, march." It is an authoritative command to move; it demands and expects obedience. Thus the Lord is pictured as. a military commander, the Captain of our salvation, who is moving out the troops under His authority.

The phrase, "the voice of the archangel," is significant because when God put His plans into operation, He frequently used angels as His emissaries and agents. Angels execute God's will. In the Old Testament the law was given through angels. In the New Testament angels ministered to Christ at His temptation and were with Him at His death. At the coming of Christ for His church, God will give orders to the chief of the angelical hierarchy, who will see that the will of God is carried out.

The phrase, "the trump of God," is significant, for in the Old Testament the trumpet was used for two things— to summon to battle and to summon to worship.

In light of the picture given in these phrases, two interpretations are possible. The shout, the voice of the archangel, and the trump of God may be the commands issued
to the angelic hosts as they are about to engage Satan in
battle to wrest the body of every believer from his dominion
and control. This will be the climax of the battle between
Christ and Satan in which Christ will be victorious.

Or perhaps the shout, the voice of the archangel, and
the trump of God are addressed to believers, not to angels,
to summon them to that great assembly where worship
and praise, honor and glory, will be given to God the
Father and the Son. In the first interpretation, Christ
would be commanding angels to "Go and liberate." In the
second interpretation, He would be commanding us to
"Come and worship." In either case, it is the authoritative
Word of God that sets the whole program in motion.

In verse 17 we have the next step. The resurrection of
dead believers (v. 15) will be followed by the catching up
of living believers. The Lord Jesus will be sent by the
Father to this earth to bring all believers of this age, both
living and dead, into His presence. When the authoritative
shout is given, the graves will open and the bodies of all
believers will come forth. As those bodies are being raised,
we who are alive will be caught up, will be glorified, and
will be joined to the group of the resurrected saints and
together we will meet the Lord in the air. This reveals that
before either group meets the Lord in the air, they are
joined into one group. There will be no distinction, no
privilege, for either group. The two—the resurrected
dead and the translated living—will be joined into one
group and they will, as one body, meet the Lord. Paul
concluded, "Wherefore comfort one another with these

words." There is comfort in these words because there will be no separation, no division, no distinction, no privilege experienced by one group that is not enjoyed by all.

This translation of believers apparently will have little effect on those left on earth. It will make little if any impression on the multitudes of the lost who are left to go into the tribulation. Their hearts have been hardened against Christ. They have rejected Him as Savior, and when they see this great sign of His authority they are totally indifferent to its significance. When the Gospel is proclaimed during the tribulation, it will fall, for the most part, on deaf ears. It requires the sovereign work of God to prepare a multitude of believing witnesses (Rev. 7) so that a multitude can hear of salvation through the blood of Christ.

But what does this promise mean to us? The passages that have to do with the translation of the church never say that Christ is coming to take us to heaven. Each time it speaks of Christ's coming it is to take us to Himself. First Thessalonians 4:17 says, "We which are alive and remain shall be caught up together with them in the clouds, to meet the Lord in the air: and so shall we ever be with the Lord." In John 14 Jesus Christ said, "If I go to prepare a place for you, I will come again, and receive you unto myself. . . ." Titus 2:13 says that we are looking for "the glorious appearing of the great God and our Saviour Jesus Christ." The glory of heaven is not in the gold of the streets, nor the jewels of the gates, nor the splendor and beauty of our habitation. The glory of heaven is the person of our Lord and Savior, Jesus Christ. We are not looking for an event nor a program. We are looking for a Person. And we can live day by day, hour by hour, and moment by moment with the expectation that the Lord may come at any time.

The promise of an imminent visit of a dear friend changes our priorities and behavior. So too the promise of an unannounced visit from the Lord to take us "home" ought to produce in us a higher quality of life as we wait for His coming.

The translation, or rapture, of the church is not some distant hope, something that may happen generations from now. It could take place at any moment. Before this day closes, the Lord could come. Before tomorrow dawns, believers might be at home in glory. How imperative it is for each individual to receive Jesus Christ as Savior lest the day of His coming should find someone unprepared. And the expectancy of Christ's return must certainly produce in us a new faithfulness. May we be found ready and faithful.

3

God's Picture of the Tribulation

Matthew 24:4–26

THE GREAT TRIBULATION is a term that strikes terror into people's hearts, and the word *Armageddon* chills the spine. People everywhere dread God's wrath. Even those with little or no knowledge of the Bible have the conviction that God must judge the earth because of its wickedness. When we look at history, we see a continuous and unbroken record of rebellion against God. Civilization after civilization and nation after nation have walked in the way of godlessness and unrighteousness, and people anticipate God's wrath as a result. And yet few are clear about what the Bible teaches concerning the tribulation.

My purpose in this chapter is to relate the tribulation period to the general panorama of the ages and to show God's purpose in it.

After His death and resurrection, the Lord Jesus Christ continued on earth for a brief period before He was taken up into glory. On the day of Pentecost, which occurred fifty days after the Passover, the Holy Spirit came to take up residence in the church, which is His body. This present age began at that time and has continued for more than nineteen hundred years.

Scripture reveals that it will end with the rapture of the church, but it does not say when. After the rapture of the church, there will be a seven-year period called the tribulation. At the end of the tribulation, the Lord will return to earth personally and visibly. This is called the Second Advent, or the Second Coming of Christ. At that time, He will institute a kingdom on earth, the Millennial Kingdom, which will last for a thousand years.

This significant seven-year era will be divided into equal parts of three and one-half years (Dan. 9:27; Rev. 11:3). The whole seven-year period is called the tribulation and is referred to as "the time of Jacob's trouble" (Jer. 20:7), "the indignation" (Isa. 26:20), and "a time of trouble" (Dan. 12:1). The last half of the period is called "the *great* tribulation" (Matt. 24:15).

We must remember that the word *tribulation* is used in the Bible in both a technical and a non-technical sense. When used non-technically, it speaks of any trial or suffering through which an individual may go. When used in its technical sense, it refers to the seven-year period following the translation of the church, a time of unprecedented judgment and wrath from God upon the earth.

One of the most extensive descriptions of this period is found in Zephaniah 1:12–18, where Zephaniah writes concerning "the day of the Lord." The day of the Lord is an extended period of time that begins after the rapture of the church and extends through the millennial age. Thus it includes both a time of judgment and a time of blessing.

In Zephaniah it is obvious that the day of the Lord refers
not to the thousand-year millennial reign of Christ—a time
of righteousness, peace, justice, and blessing—but rather
to the time of judgment, the tribulation. The prophet
describes it as a day of wrath, trouble, distress, waste,
desolation, gloominess, clouds and darkness, alarm, and
death. That certainly is not an inviting picture. We can go
through every passage in the Bible dealing with the tribulation and not find a single word that alleviates or miti-
gates the suffering, misery, and the visitation of God's
wrath poured out on the earth.

In Matthew 24 we have Christ's own description of this
period. In verses 4–8 He described the events of the first
half of the period and in verses 9–14 the last half. Then
He summed it up by saying, "for then shall be great
tribulation, such as was not since the beginning of the
world to this time, no, nor ever shall be. And except those
days should be shortened [or terminated], there should no
flesh be saved . . ." (v. 21). The Lord Jesus announced
that the tribulation will be so destructive that if God did
not bring it to an end, every living thing would be destroyed. But God will bring the period to a close because
He has a purpose to accomplish through living individuals
during the millennial age.

John, in Revelation, gave the most extensive description
of the suffering of the tribulation. "The great day of his
wrath is come" (6:17). He referred to the "wine of the
wrath of God" and the "winepress of the wrath of God"
(14:10, 19). Vials full of the "wrath of God" will be poured
out on the earth (15:7; 16:1). All nations shall taste of the
"cup of the wine of the fierceness of his wrath" (16:19).
John portrayed the period as a time of judgment (14:7;

15:4; 16:7). So intense is the suffering that, according to Revelation 6:15–17, "The kings of the earth, and the great men, and the rich men, and the chief captains, and the mighty men, and every bondman, and every free man, hid themselves in the dens and in the rocks of the mountains; and said to the mountains and rocks, 'Fall on us, and hide us from the face of him that sitteth on the throne, and from the wrath of the Lamb; For the great day of his wrath is come; and who shall be able to stand?'"

Here we have one of the greatest prayers that has ever gone up from the face of the earth. People are praying for the rocks and the mountains to fall on them and destroy them because of the fierceness of God's wrath. No matter where we go in the Word, Scripture designates the character of this period as darkness, judgment, pain, suffering, woe, warfare, bloodshed, wrath, and death.

The book of Revelation discusses the sequence of events that will take place in the tribulation. In Revelation 6 we find One seated on a throne who holds in His hand a scroll. It has been written upon, then rolled and sealed. This has been repeated seven times. John watches the Lord Jesus Christ open this seven-sealed book. This scroll reveals the first series of judgments to be poured out upon the earth by God. They cover the events of the first half of the tribulation. In verses 1 and 2 we see a rider on a white horse. This refers to a great false peace movement that brings the world under the authority of one ruler. His role will be developed later when we study the rise of the Roman Empire in its final form. In verses 3 and 4 we see a rider on a red horse, to whom power was given "to take peace from the earth, and that they should kill one another." This is worldwide warfare. In verses 5 and 6, as the third seal is opened, we see worldwide famine, poverty, and want. In verses 7 and 8, under the fourth seal, is a widespread visitation of death that follows the warfare, famine, and pestilence of the former seals. John is describing the worldwide suffering of the first three and one-half years of the tribulation.

In Matthew 24 the Lord Jesus described this same period. "And Jesus answered and said unto them, 'Take heed that no man deceive you. For many shall come in my name, saying, "I am Christ" [the rider of the white horse]; And ye shall hear of wars and rumours of wars [the rider of the red horse]: For nation shall rise against nation, and kingdom against kingdom: and there shall be famines, and pestilences, and earthquakes in divers places [the rider on the black horse]'" (vv. 4–7). And all these things are only the "beginning of sorrows" (v. 8), that is, the false labor pains that warn of the impending birth of the new age that Christ is going to institute on earth when He comes.

In Revelation 8–10 we have John's description of the events of the last three and one-half years of the tribulation. In symbolic language he explained more of the visitation of God's wrath to be poured out upon the earth. This time, instead of portraying it as a sealed scroll, he used the figure of trumpets blowing to sound an alarm. The first trumpet blows and there is hail and fire mingled with blood that burns up one-third of all the earth, trees, and grass (v. 7). This seems to be a divine visitation of judgment upon nature. As God cursed the earth, the scene of man's first sin, so God curses the earth, the scene of man's greatest manifestation of lawlessness. At the sounding of the second trumpet, a great mountain like a volcano erupts into the sea and one-third of the sea becomes blood (vv.

8–9). The whole course of precipitation is upset so that famine, want, and death result. The third trumpet sounds, and John sees a great star fall from heaven and darken one-third of the sun, moon, and stars (vv. 12–13), leaving a supernatural darkness over the face of the earth. The fifth trumpet introduces a horde of locusts that disseminate death over the face of the earth (9:1–12). The sixth trumpet reveals a marching army of two hundred million men who destroy one-third of the world's population as they pass across the earth (9:13–21).

These chapters describe events so gigantic and stupendous that we can hardly conceive of them. Yet that is God's picture of His wrath upon the earth during the last half of the tribulation. As bad as this picture is, even more follows. In Revelation 16, using the figure of vials, or bowls, John explains again the wrath of God as a series of events that take place in a very short time, perhaps within a few days at the end of the tribulation.

While the seals cover the first three and one-half years and the trumpets the last three and one-half, the vials cover just a short period of time, thereby portraying a special manifestation of divine judgment and wrath. Through the judgment of the first vial (v. 2), there comes a great running, festering sore upon the body of every man who gave allegiance to the Beast and the False Prophet. Through the second vial (v. 3), the sea is again turned to blood, bringing worldwide death. The third vial (v. 4) turns the rivers and waters to blood, causing famine and thirst. The fourth vial (v. 8) makes the sun so hot that it scorches men with fire. Evidently the relationship between the sun and the earth is so altered that the sun burns all that is alive. The fifth vial (v. 10) brings judg-

ment upon all those who are in the kingdom of the Beast.
They gnaw their tongues for pain and blaspheme the God
of heaven because of their suffering. In the sixth vial (v.
12) we find again a great army that comes from the East
and marches toward Palestine, leaving death in its wake.
With the emptying of the seventh vial (v. 17), we see the
final display of God's wrath.

"Why would God do such things?" we ask. A God who
would pour out such wrath upon the earth must not be a
God of love, we conclude. "Why is God going to judge the
world?"

We ask these questions and come to these conclusions
because we have such a limited concept of the holiness
of God and the unholiness of man. We understand little about God's attitude toward rebellion and rebellious
ones. God gave these prophecies to us so that we might
realize His hatred for sin and His judgment on sinners and
upon the scene of their sins. This revelation shows us
God's concept of the enormity of the sin of rejecting
Christ.

God reveals several purposes for bringing tribulation
upon the earth. There is a purpose in reference to the
nation Israel; a purpose in reference to the Gentile nations;
a purpose in reference to God's dealing with Satan; and a
purpose in reference to sinners themselves.

The Nation Israel

When Jesus began His public ministry, His first spoken
words were, "Repent, for the kingdom of heaven is at
hand" (Matt. 4:17). He came unto His own people to call
them to repentance, to offer them the promised kingdom,
to bring the promised blessings of redemption to them.

The nation Israel watched with interest as the Lord Jesus lived His life before them. They followed Him avidly as He worked miracle after miracle and gave them sign after sign that He was the Messiah. They listened as words flowed from His lips declaring that He had come to reveal God to them and that He was of divine, not human, origin.

But when the Lord began to press His message home, to remind them that they would have no fellowship with Him and no part in His kingdom unless they turned from their sins and accepted Him as Messiah, they rejected Him. They accused Him before Pilate of being a traitor because He had presented Himself as "Jesus of Nazareth, the King of the Jews," and Pilate condemned Him to death. The sin of the nation Israel in rejecting Christ was not a sin of ignorance; it was a willful sin. Thus the Lord Jesus announced judgment upon the nation. He said, "O Jerusalem, Jerusalem, thou that killest the prophets, and stonest them which are sent unto thee, how often would I have gathered thy children together, even as a hen gathereth her chickens under her wings, and ye would not! Behold, your house is left to you desolate. For I say unto you, Ye shall not see me henceforth, till ye shall say, 'Blessed is he that cometh in the name of the Lord'" (Matt. 23:37–39). This announcement gives us the key to understanding Israel's present day suffering and to interpreting the purpose of God in reference to Israel in the tribulation, a time of judgment on a nation that willfully rejected Jesus Christ.

The purpose of God for Israel in the tribulation is further revealed in Ezekiel 20:33–38. There God says that He will bring back into the land a people who have been scattered, and will cause them to pass under the rod of judgment. He will purge out the rebels and leave a believing remnant with whom He can fulfill all the promises of the kingdom. Thus, as far as Israel is concerned, the tribulation will bring judgment on the unbelievers in the nation because of the sin of rejecting Christ, and will bring salvation and blessing on those who turn to Him in that day.

The Gentile Nations

In the time of Nebuchadnezzar, a Gentile nation captured the land of Palestine. That land has been under a succession of Gentile rulers from the time of Nebuchadnezzar—more than five hundred years before Christ—to the present day. Palestine was ruled by the Babylonians, then by the Medo-Persians, then by the Grecians, and then by the many different forms of the Roman Empire.

During the tribulation period, Israel once again will be ruled by the Roman Empire. But God is going to judge those Gentile nations because they have oppressed Israel. In Matthew 25:31–46 the Lord spoke of the judgment that separates sheep from goats. This is a judgment on living Gentiles. At the time of His return, the Lord will separate all Gentiles into two classes—the saved and the unsaved. To the saved, the sheep, the Lord will say, "Come, ye blessed of my Father, inherit the kingdom prepared for you from the foundation of the world" (Matt. 25:34). To the unsaved, the goats, He will say, "Depart from me, ye cursed, into everlasting fire, prepared for the devil and his angels" (Matt. 25:41). This judgment will remove every unsaved Gentile, for God is going to pour out fury upon Gentile people who have sought to thwart God's purpose by exterminating Israel.

In Revelation 3:10 John wrote, "Because thou hast kept the word of my patience, I also will keep thee from the hour of temptation, which shall come upon all the world, to try them that dwell upon the earth." The tribulation here is viewed as a test of those who dwell upon the earth. The phrase *dwell upon the earth* or *earth-dweller* does not speak of a geographical location. Rather it is an ethical word that speaks of those who belong to or are joined to the earth. We would call them "earthlings." Here John shows that the Lord Jesus Christ is going to pour out His fury on the earthlings to prove which people are truly His own and which really belong to the earth.

Satan

The third purpose God will accomplish through the tribulation is the revelation of Satan's true program and character and to permit his system to come to its logical end. Before the creation of the world, Satan rebelled against God's authority because he wanted to be the head of a kingdom. He wanted to rule over every created intelligence and to take the authority that belongs to God alone and to exercise it. But his system is lawless. God has put a control upon Satan's system and said, "You can go so far, but no further." In spite of all the wickedness and godlessness in the world today, we haven't seen a fraction of what the lawlessness of Satan actually is. And we have seen only a little of how evil the human heart actually is because God is restraining Satan so that his kingdom cannot come to its full manifestation in this present age (2 Thess. 2:7).

But during the tribulation God is going to say to Satan, "You have wanted to demonstrate what your kingdom is like without restraints or hindrances, but I have always restrained you. Now I'm going to take the restraint away and let you have your own way in the earth." Then this earth is going to see a reign of lawlessness never even imagined, let alone experienced. Under the power of Satan the world will be brought under the rule of the Beast, who will be the head of the Federated States of Europe (Rev. 13:1–10). Paul described this in 2 Thessalonians 2 when he wrote, "that man of sin (shall) be revealed, the son of perdition; who opposeth and exalteth himself above all that is called God, or that is worshipped; so that he as God sitteth in the temple of God, shewing himself that he is God." Through the rule of this one, the lawlessness of Satan will be openly and fully demonstrated. Sin will have its manifestation; lawlessness will have its full display.

Sinners

The final purpose to be accomplished in the tribulation is judgment upon sinners themselves, to punish them for rejecting the Gospel. So great will be their suffering that they will seek physical death and not find it (Rev. 6:16). In spite of the suffering, they continue in their rejection and impenitence. They "blasphemed the God of heaven because of their pains and their sores, and repented not [or, as the Greek says, they would not repent] of their deeds" (16:11). Although opportunity is given to repent, they refuse the offer of grace and continue their worship of Satan. God will bring judgment upon people who have gone off into this spiritual harlotry, worshiping Satan as their god.

Thus we see these purposes of God fulfilled in the tribulation: (1) to purge the nation Israel and bring a remnant to Himself; (2) to punish the Gentiles because of their despicable treatment of the Jews; (3) to reveal the true character of Satan's kingdom; (4) to punish unbelievers for their rejection of Christ.

During the tribulation, according to Revelation 7, God will raise up witnesses to His grace. Like Paul on the Damascus way, they will be brought out of darkness into light by the sovereign act of God. So God will lay hold of 144,000 Jews and will send them over the face of the earth to announce salvation through the blood of Christ (Rev. 7:14). Multitudes from "all nations, and kindreds, and people, and tongues" (Rev. 7:9) will meet the Lord when He comes back to earth to reign. The majority of those who accept Jesus Christ as Savior during the tribulation will pay with their lives for their faith in Him, because Satan will try to exterminate every believer on the face of the earth through the reign of the Beast and the False Prophet.

Praise God, we are not dreading the tribulation. We are not wondering when the events of the seals, the trumpets, and the vials will burst upon the world. For the Lord has given us the blessed hope that before God lets these events unfold on the earth, He will appear in the clouds and summon every believer to Himself. When God's wrath is poured out upon the earth and upon earthlings, we will be in His presence, for "there is therefore now no condemnation [judgment] to them which are in Christ Jesus" (Rom. 8:1). We have His promise that He has "delivered us from the wrath to come" (1 Thess. 1:10). We have a living, victorious, triumphant Savior, who will receive us and bring us deliverance from the hour of testing that is coming upon the earth.

4

The Church and the Tribulation

1 Thessalonians 5:1–11

FEW, IF ANY, prophetic questions are more vigorously debated than whether or not the church will go through the tribulation. Some say the church is going through all seven years of the tribulation. Others say the church will go through the first half only. Still others hold that the church will not go through any portion of it. And some even say that sanctified believers will be taken out before the tribulation begins and the rest of the church will be left to experience the judgment.

The problem that faces the student of prophecy is the relationship of time between the translation of the church and the tribulation. In other words, are we waiting for the man of sin, for the great world war that will wipe out millions of people, for the great world dictator, for the religious system of the False Prophet, or for the Son of God who will translate us out of this earth before these events transpire? What is our hope?

I once had the privilege of teaching the doctrine of future things in what was then the Philadelphia Bible Institute. It was my earnest conviction then, as now, that the church would not go through any part of the tribulation. On a day when I was preparing to give the class my reasons for holding that position, a visitor came into my classroom and asked permission to sit in on the lecture. I consented. Midway through the lecture, the visitor challenged my position with a question. Because it was my responsibility to teach the students rather than debate strangers, I declined to answer during class time but said I would talk with him after class. As soon as I dismissed the class he made his way to me and said that he believed the church *would* go through the tribulation.

"My blessed hope is that the Lord Jesus Christ will appear in the heavens and take me to Himself before the judgments of the tribulation begin. I live in the light of that hope daily," I said to him. "Tell me, what is your blessed hope?"

To my amazement, he replied, "I confidently expect to be martyred under the reign of the Beast."

"Do you mean to tell me," I asked, "that that is a blessed hope?"

We have been given a glorious hope, but just what is it?

First, let's consider the partial rapture position. This view holds that when the Lord Jesus Christ comes in the clouds to take the church to Himself, the only ones translated will be those who have had some second work of grace. They believe the Body of Christ will be divided into two parts at the rapture—the sanctified, who will go to be with the Lord, and the unsanctified, who will be left on earth to go through the tribulation as a kind of Protestant purgatory.

I reject this interpretation, even though it is held by some very devout people, because God's Word says that the death of Christ removes all sin: "Their sins and iniquities will I remember no more" (Heb. 10:17). The death of Christ gives believers a standing before God so that we are perfectly acceptable to God. There is no reason the blood-washed ones cannot be received into God's presence, for they have been robed in the righteousness of Christ. The blood of Christ gives eternal life and salvation as a free and gracious gift to all who accept Christ as Savior. Because of the finished work of Christ, there is not a single reason why God should keep any believer out of heaven at the time of the rapture. The value of the finished work of Christ makes a partial rapture impossible.

Further, the unity of the Body of Christ makes a partial rapture impossible. God is calling out a people whom He will give to His Son as His bride. If the partial rapture view is correct, the bride presented by the Father to the Son will have some body parts missing. Everyone who has accepted Christ as personal Savior has been made a member of the Body of Christ by the work of the Holy Spirit (1 Cor. 12:13) and will be a part of the bride presented by the Father to the Son.

This doctrine also makes our own works, or our own righteousness, the basis for our translation and our blessed hope. God will not accept anyone into heaven whose hope rests on something other than the work of Christ.

Second, the teaching that we call the post-tribulation rapture position holds that the church will go through the seven years of the tribulation, endure the judgment of the wrath of God, and then be caught up to meet the Lord in the air to return immediately with Him to earth.

People who believe this do not deny that there will be a rapture, but they hold that it will take place after the tribulation.

To prove this they use such Scripture passages as John 15:18–19, where Jesus said, "If the world hate you, ye know that it hated me before it hated you. If ye were of the world, the world would love his own: but because ye are not of the world, but I have chosen you out of the world, therefore the world hateth you." They also use John 16:33, "In the world ye shall have tribulation. . . ."

In the Upper Room discourse the Lord Jesus warned the disciples they would suffer tribulation for His name's sake. But the word *tribulation* is used in two different senses in the Bible. It is used in reference to that seven-year period of judgment upon the earth. But it is also used for any severe trial that comes upon individuals who live in finite bodies in a world that is antagonistic to Christ. In this sense believers must expect tribulation in general, but we were never told we must endure the seven-year tribulation.

The third view, called the mid-tribulation rapture position, says that the church will go through the first three and one-half years of the seven-year tribulation but will be raptured before the second half begins. During the first half of the tribulation, there will be wars, pestilence, famine, disease, desolation, and death as the beginning of God's wrath is poured out on the earth. For the same reasons the church cannot go through the complete tribulation, neither can it go through the first part, for the first half is also a time of judgment.

The fourth view is called the pre-tribulation rapture. It says that the church will be translated *before* any of the tribulation begins. I believe this to be true for several reasons.

First, the very nature of the tribulation period—wrath, judgment, indignation, darkness, destruction, and death—contradicts Christ's promises to believers. "There is therefore now no condemnation [judgment] to them which are in Christ Jesus" (Rom. 8:1). From 1 John 4:17 we learn that when it comes to judgment "as he is, so are we in this world." As Christ cannot be punished again for the sins of the world, neither can we be brought into judgment for sin. The church cannot undergo the visitation of God because there is *no* judgment for her. The church has been cleansed, purchased, and set apart for Jesus Christ. The church is Christ's body, and He is the Head. God will not permit the redeemed to go through that period of judgment.

But some will say, "Haven't saints always had to suffer? Don't saints need to be cleansed?" That certainly is true. We need cleansing daily. But God's method of cleansing His children who become defiled is not to send them through the fire of judgment. God's method of cleansing sinful saints is through the blood of Jesus Christ. God will not set aside the blood of Christ and use the fires of judgment as His cleansing agent. Thus the very nature of the tribulation prevents the church from going through it.

Second, the purposes of the tribulation prevent the church from going through it. These purposes, outlined in a previous chapter, are to purify Israel, to punish Gentile nations for their treatment of God's people and God's Gospel, to manifest the lawlessness of the Satanic kingdom, and to judge sinners. These purposes are totally unrelated to the church. God is not dealing with the church in the tribulation period, but is terminating His program with Israel, Gentiles, Satan, and sinners.

Third, when the Lord Jesus returns to this earth to reign, there must be believers on the earth for Him to take into His kingdom. If the rapture occurs at the end of the tribulation, immediately before His return to earth, and removes all believers, there would be no one on earth at the time of the Second Advent over whom the King could reign. There must be some interval of time between the rapture and the Second Advent to win the believers who will be the subjects of the earthly millennial reign of Christ.

One of the major passages about this is Paul's letter to believers in Thessalonica who misunderstood his teaching. They were experiencing great persecution and had begun to wonder, "Could these persecutions be the tribulation? If so, what about Paul's teachings that the church would not go through that period?" Doubt had been raised by some reports, supposedly from Paul himself, affirming that they were then in the tribulation. The people wanted to know two things: (1) Are the persecutions we are enduring those of the tribulation, and (2) Was Paul right when he taught us that we would not go through the tribulation?

In 2 Thessalonians 2:1, Paul responded to their questions. "We beseech you, brethren, by the coming of our Lord Jesus Christ, and by our gathering together unto him, that ye be not soon shaken in mind, or be troubled, neither by spirit, nor by word, nor by letter as from us, as that the day of Christ [or better, the day of the Lord] is at hand [or better, has already come]." Thus he answered the first question, "Are we in the tribulation?" He said they were not. Then he gave proof: "that day shall not come, except there come a falling away first, and that man of sin be revealed, the son of perdition" (v. 3). The "falling away" or "departure" could be either the departure from the faith in the last days or the departure of the saints from the earth. Either view does not alter the argument. Paul said they could know they were not in the day of the Lord because this departure had not taken place, neither had the man of sin been revealed.

This man of sin is the head of the Federated States of Europe, the final form of Gentile world power. As long as this individual, who will rule the world as a god under Satan's authority, has not appeared, we know we are not in the tribulation.

The reason that individual has not yet appeared is clearly stated: "For the mystery of the iniquity [lawlessness] doth already work: only he who now letteth [hinders] will let [keep on hindering], until he be taken out of the way" (v. 7). Paul stated that Satan was being restrained from dominating the world through his masterpiece—the imitator of Christ. But who is restraining Satan? Some believe it is the law principle; some say it is human government; others believe it is the church. It is my conviction that the Restrainer is the Holy Spirit, who has made the church His temple.

When the Lord Jesus appears in the heaven to remove the church from the world, God's restraint will be removed and Satan will then rise to a position of world domination. This suggests that the tribulation cannot begin until the church has been translated.

Another consideration is found in Revelation 4. After describing the seven-fold condition of the visible church in chapters 2 and 3, John wrote, "And round about the throne were four and twenty seats [or thrones]; and upon the seats I saw four and twenty elders sitting, clothed in white raiment; and they had on their heads crowns of gold" (v. 4). These elders are significant because they are *seated*, robed, and crowned. This suggests that these twenty-four are the symbolic representation of the church. In Ephesians 2:6 we read that God has "made us *sit* together in heavenly places in Jesus Christ." Revelation 19:8 states, "And to her was granted that she should be arrayed in fine linen, clean and white: for the fine linen is the righteousness of saints." Again in 2 Timothy 4:8, Paul testified, "Henceforth there is laid up for me a crown of righteousness, which the Lord, the righteous judge, shall give me at that day: and not to me only, but unto all them also that love his appearing." These considerations seem to identify the twenty-four elders as the church, and they were seen in heaven in their glorified position at the outset of the tribulation. To be seen and described by John in Revelation 4–19, their rapture must have preceded the tribulation.

This same truth is taught in Revelation 3:10. The Lord addressed a letter to the church in Philadelphia, the true church of the last days. He said to these believers, "Because thou hast kept the word of my patience, I also will keep thee from the hour of temptation, which shall come upon all the world, to try them that dwell upon the earth." The phrase *hour of temptation* can be translated "hour of testing" and is a reference to the tribulation. This is a promise of deliverance from the time of testing. Shadrach, Meshach, and Abednego, when cast into the fiery furnace, were preserved *through* the flames. Some have said that the church, in like manner, will be preserved through the tribulation. But this is not what the Lord promised. He said, "I will keep you from the time or from the very hour when the tribulation comes." His method of "keeping them from the hour" was to remove them from the place where the testing would occur. We have here a very clear promise to the church that He will keep us away from the time when the tribulation comes upon the world.

This truth is presented in 1 Thessalonians 5 also. After Paul had written those familiar words describing the translation of the church in chapter 4, he said, "But of the times and the seasons, brethren, ye have no need that I write unto you. For you yourselves know perfectly that the day of the Lord [the tribulation] so cometh as a thief in the night" (1 Thess. 5:1–2). The coming of a thief is unexpected and unannounced. No thief sends a letter announcing that he will arrive tomorrow night at midnight.

Paul used this illustration to show that it would be foolish for him to try to tell them when the tribulation would begin, because it would arrive as unexpectedly as a thief. He added that the question was of no vital concern to them anyway, for "ye, brethren, are not in darkness, that that day should overtake you as a thief. Ye are all the children of light, and the children of the day: we are not of the night nor of darkness" (vv. 4–5). This is a period for those in darkness, and since we are in the light, it does not concern us. He further affirmed, "God hath not appointed us to wrath, but to obtain salvation by our Lord Jesus Christ" (v. 9).

The wrath he had in mind was the wrath of the tribulation. The salvation he mentioned was not salvation from sin received as a gift of God's grace, but the salvation from the tribulation by translation. Thus Paul argued that since we are children of light, and the tribulation is for the children of darkness, we will not see the tribulation but will be delivered out of it by the rapture.

We see the same truth affirmed in 2 Thessalonians 1:9–10. There Paul again stated that God has delivered us from the wrath to come. Paul described the wrath he had in mind when he said, "And to you who are troubled rest with us, when the Lord Jesus shall be revealed from heaven with his mighty angels, in flaming fire taking vengeance on them that know not God, and that obey not the gospel of our Lord Jesus Christ. . . ." (2 Thess. 1:7–8). His wrath will be poured out at the second coming of the Lord Jesus to the earth. It is this wrath from which we will be delivered by translation.

An incident in Genesis 19 illustrates this truth. God had announced His plan to destroy the cities of Sodom and Gomorrah because of their wickedness and godlessness. A messenger was sent to warn Lot of this judgment and to tell him to flee Sodom. According to 2 Peter 2:7, Lot was a righteous man, and God would not judge the wicked cities until the righteous one had been removed. The presence of Lot, one righteous man, held back God's wrath from the wicked cities. Therefore Lot had to be removed before the judgment could come.

This world will see the outpouring of the wrath of God upon it in the tribulation. But as long as the church, the redeemed ones, are on the earth, judgment is stayed. Not until the church has been removed by translation will the judgment fall. After the translation of the church, when only ungodly people are left on the earth, tribulation of unprecedented force will burst upon the world.

5

Israel's Title Deed to Palestine

Genesis 12:1–9

THERE IS NO PROBLEM more perplexing to those responsible for affairs of state than what to do about the nation Israel. If someone could amicably settle the Arab-Israeli dispute, he or she would be recognized as having the wisdom of Solomon and would be considered a diplomat without equal in the history of the world.

The eyes of the world focus on the Near East. We know not when, nor by what pretext, another great world conflagration may be set off by the Arab-Israeli dispute. Heads of state debate the issue: To whom does Palestine actually belong? To the Arabs, who have been there for generations? Or to the descendants of Abraham, who first entered the land and whose descendants conquered it, possessed it for centuries, and then were driven out?

From the time of creation to the call of Abraham, God dealt with all people alike, recognizing no national distinctions or privileges. Everyone was on the same level before

Him, and revelation was made by God to all, without regard to race or geographical location. After the flood, which destroyed all human life except Noah and his family, God revealed Himself to Noah, who then spread the knowledge of God over the face of the repopulated earth. People rebelled against the revelation God gave them, however, and raised up gods for themselves.

Against this background of rejection God chose Abraham to raise up a new nation through which God could make Himself known. God did not choose someone well acquainted with His revelation, nor one who worshiped Jehovah as the true God. Instead He went to a very worldly-wise but God-rejecting city, Ur, and to the home of an idolater (Josh. 24:2). God attracted Abraham from his idolatrous family, from an idolatrous city, and separated him unto Himself.

When God called Abraham, He gave him a promise of personal blessings, national blessings, and universal blessings. The words, "I will bless them that bless thee, and curse him that curseth thee" (Gen. 12:3), contain *personal* blessings. "I will make of thee a great nation, and I will bless thee, and make thy name great; and thou shalt be a blessing" (Gen. 12:2) holds *national* promises. And "in thee shall all families of the earth be blessed" (Gen. 12:3) makes a promise that is *universal* in scope.

After Abraham received this promise from God, he departed from Ur of the Chaldees and came to the northern border of the land of Palestine, which God was going to give him. Accompanying him was his wife, Sarah, his father, Terah, and his nephew, Lot. According to Genesis 11:31–32, God halted the procession at the border of the land of Canaan and did not let them then enter the land.

God told Abraham to get out from under the authority of his idolatrous father and to leave his residence. So Abraham stayed outside the land of Palestine until his father died. After his father's death, Abraham again started on his journey and came into the land of Palestine (Gen. 12:4–5). There the Lord appeared unto him again and said, "Unto thy seed will I give this land" (Gen. 12:7).

This promise was reiterated and reaffirmed many times in God's dealing with Abraham and his descendants. In Genesis 13 we read about dissension between Abraham's and Lot's herdsmen. As a result Lot was separated from his uncle. God was bringing Abraham to the place He had previously spoken of now that he was separated from his father's country, his father's house, and his kindred.

Following the separation from Lot, God said, "Lift up now thine eyes, and look from the place where thou art northward, and southward, and eastward and westward: For all the land which thou seest, to thee will I give it, and to thy seed for ever. . . . Arise, walk through the land in the length of it and in the breadth of it; for I will give it unto thee" (Gen. 13:14–15, 17). Abraham was in that separated place where God could bless him, and God appeared again to reaffirm that which He had promised— that the land belonged to Abraham and his seed forever.

In Genesis 14 we learn about a coalition of kings who conquered the cities of Sodom and Gomorrah. Lot had taken up residence in Sodom. When Sodom fell into the hands of this coalition, led by Chedorlaomer, Lot was captured. Abraham vanquished Chedorlaomer and the coalition of kings and delivered Lot. The king of Sodom, out of gratitude, offered Abraham all the spoils of conquest, thus conferring great riches on the deliverer. But

Abraham refused to take anything the king offered (Gen. 14:23–24). Abraham had God's promise of protection and provision, and he trusted God to fulfill His promise. In response to this trust, God again spoke to Abraham saying, "Fear not, Abram: I am thy shield, and thy exceeding great reward" (Gen. 15:1).

When God reminded Abraham of His faithfulness, Abraham took courage to remind God that He had promised him an heir. At that time the closest thing Abraham had to an heir was a stranger who managed his household. God strengthened Abraham's faith by promising him a seed as multitudinous as the stars of heaven (Gen. 15:5). To this Abraham replied with a trusting "Amen." "He believed in the Lord" (Gen. 15:6). On the basis of this affirmation, Abraham was declared righteous (Rom. 4:3).

To this one declared righteous by faith, God said, "I am the Lord that brought thee out of Ur of the Chaldees, to give thee this land to inherit it" (Gen. 15:7). The previous promise of God is reiterated and is now to be confirmed through the strongest possible affirmation, the blood covenant.

In Old Testament times there were three ways to secure a contract—a shoe covenant, a salt covenant, and a blood covenant. The most common method of confirming any agreement was the shoe covenant, in which the two parties would exchange sandals, something of value because they were necessary for travel. When Boaz was going to redeem Ruth, he removed his shoe before the judges and gave it to the one who had the first right to redeem Ruth. Boaz was entering into a shoe covenant (Ruth 4:7).

The second and more binding covenant was the salt covenant (Num. 18:19; Lev. 2:13; 2 Chron 13:5). Salt was even more important than sandals, especially for those who traveled the deserts. It was vital for life. Travelers carried leather pouches of salt to meet their needs. When two would be bound together in a contract more secure than a shoe covenant, each would take a pinch of salt from the other's pouch and place it in his own. Then they would shake the pouches. The contract founded on the salt covenant could be broken only when each received his own pinch of salt again. Since this was impossible, the salt covenant was considered a most binding contract.

The third covenant was the blood covenant. In this form of covenant, the contracting parties would slay an animal, divide the carcass down the backbone, and place the divided parts opposite each other on the ground to form a pathway between the pieces. The two would join hands, recite the terms of the contract, and walk together between the divided halves of the slain animal. This signified that they were bound in a contract until death, and if either violated the terms of the contract, his blood would be poured out as the blood of the animal had been poured out.

God called on Abraham to prepare the animal that would make a blood covenant possible. God was about to confirm His promise to Abraham with a blood covenant. Because of the large number of animals God required for this ritual, when one would have been sufficient, Abraham surely realized the great significance attached to what was happening. Abraham slew the heifer, the goat, the ram, and the birds and laid their carcasses on the ground, preparing to enter into this blood covenant about which he and God had been speaking.

At this point in the ritual, God caused Abraham to fall into a deep sleep so that he could not participate in the ritual personally. In his sleep, Abraham saw "a smoking furnace, and a burning lamp that passed between those pieces" (Gen. 15:17). In the Old Testament the burning lamp, or the light, signified the presence of the Shekinah glory of God. God Himself, apart from Abraham's participation or promise, was binding Himself by a blood covenant to fulfill what He had promised to Abraham.

The terms of the covenant were clearly stated, "In the same day the Lord made a covenant with Abram, saying, 'Unto thy seed have I given this land. . . .'" (Gen. 15:18). The dimensions of the land are clearly stated, stretching from the Nile to the Euphrates and from the Arabian peninsula to Asia Minor. In no clearer way could God signify to Abraham and Abraham's descendants that Palestine was their God-given possession forever.

When we turn to the present position of Israel, we find that the nation, though promised the land of Palestine, is not in real possession of it. Why? Some believe that the covenant made by God that gave Israel the land of Palestine was a conditional covenant and depended upon the obedience of Abraham's descendants for its fulfillment. They contend that if Israel did not obey, God would forget His covenant and abrogate His promise. Although God promised chastisement for disobedience, He nowhere indicated that His covenant could ever be set aside.

In this connection, Deuteronomy 28–30 is very important, for it outlines God's dealing with Israel and explains Israel's present position. The children of Israel had been out of the land of Palestine for more than four hundred years when Moses delivered the message in Deuteronomy 28. The land itself was again in the possession of Israel's enemies, who sought to bar her readmission to the land.

The redeemed nation, delivered from Egypt under Moses, was approaching the land of milk and honey under Joshua, only to find it a land flowing with strong enemies. Moses' message was given to strengthen Joshua and the people as they faced the task of re-entering Palestine. They had many questions: Do we still have any rights there? Does that land still belong to us? Do we have the right to occupy it? Will God be with us? Or has He forsaken us and forgotten His promise?

Moses assured them that even a four-hundred-year absence could not abrogate the promise of God. In Deuteronomy 28:1–14 God promised blessing for obedience, and in 28:15–47 He promised cursing and judgment for disobedience. Following this, Moses prophesied the future Assyrian and Babylonian captivities and also the Roman captivity as God's judgment for disobedience (Deut. 28:47–62). The judgment of God would take the form of captivity and expulsion from the land of promise (Deut. 28:63–68). "The Lord shall scatter thee among all people, from the end of the earth even unto the other. . . ." (Deut. 28:64).

The books of Kings and Chronicles record the apostasy and idolatry of the nation Israel. The people to whom God had revealed Himself, to whom He had given His love, for whom He had instituted the Tabernacle as a center of worship, to whom He had given Aaron and his sons for priests as a means of access to Himself, had gotten so far into idolatry that they set up an image and offered infants in human sacrifice. They followed the religious system instituted by Jezebel, setting up idols in every grove, worshiping the sun, moon, and stars. According to His established principle of justice, God moved the nation out of their land into Assyrian and Babylonian captivities.

When Christ came unto His own to be acclaimed as Messiah "His own received him not." When He presented Himself, the Jews cried, "Away with him, away with him . . . we have no king but Caesar" (John 19:15). Consequently, Christ pronounced judgment on that nation: "And they shall fall by the edge of the sword, and shall be led away captive into all nations: and Jerusalem shall be trodden down of the Gentiles, until the times of the Gentiles be fulfilled" (Luke 21:24).

The judgment for their rejection was expulsion from the land and destruction of their beloved city, Jerusalem. Israel today is experiencing the expulsion that Moses spoke of in Deuteronomy 28 and that Christ spoke of in Matthew 23 and Luke 21. When Nebuchadnezzar destroyed Jerusalem in 586 B.C. Israel was removed from the land and Palestine passed into the control of non-Jewish people. It remains so today.

What about the future of Israel? Will she ever again occupy her promised land? A great body of Scripture tells of a future regathering and restoration of the Jews to Palestine. The prophet Daniel spoke of the destruction of Jerusalem and the sanctuary in that city (Dan. 9:26), the same event described by the Lord Jesus (Matt. 24 and Luke 21), which was accomplished in 70 A.D. by the Roman legions under Titus. Daniel 9:27 speaks of one who will arise on the world's scene and confirm a covenant with many (Israel) for one week (seven years).

When God brings this age (the age of the church) to a close with the translation of the church, the tribulation will begin. According to 2 Thessalonians 2, it will begin with a public appearance by the man of sin, the head of the Federated States of Europe. He will assert his authority by trying to settle the Arab-Israeli dispute. He will side with Israel, backing her claim to the land of Palestine against Russia, or the Northern confederacy, who will back the Arabs' claim to Palestine (Ezek. 38). This head of the European confederacy will make a contract with Israel, guaranteeing protection against any aggressor. In the security of this pledge, the Jews will go back to the land in unprecedented numbers.

When they are in the land, enjoying a time of peace and prosperity under the protection of the European confederacy, Israel will look to the west and conclude that this man of sin, who claims to have fulfilled the Abrahamic covenant, is indeed God and will give him worship that belongs to Jehovah alone. God will not tolerate this situation and will let army after army move into Palestine to drive the Jews out of their land. Two-thirds of the Jews will perish, again drenching the soil of Palestine with the blood of the children of Abraham (Zech. 13:8), and the majority of those left behind will flee. The prophecy of Moses will have its ultimate fulfillment: "And among these nations shalt thou find no ease, neither shall the sole of thy foot have rest: but the Lord shall give thee there a trembling heart, and failing of eyes, and sorrow of mind: And thy life shall hang in doubt before thee; and thou shalt fear day and night, and shalt have none assurance of thy life: In the morning thou shalt say, Would God it were morning! for the fear of thine heart wherewith thou shalt fear, and for the sight of thine eyes which thou shalt see" (Deut. 28:65–67).

In spite of this unbelief, God will call out from among that nation a multitude of witnesses to His grace. God will do 144,000 times over what He did for Saul on the

Damascus road, and He will bring to Himself a remnant in Israel who will go to the ends of the earth to proclaim salvation through the blood of Christ.

When the Lord returns to earth, He will come as King of kings and Lord of lords to put down every enemy and to reign. At that time God will regather the nation Israel back to their land. Christ spoke of this when He said, "Immediately after the tribulation of those days shall the sun be darkened, and the moon shall not give her light, and the stars shall fall from heaven, and the powers of the heavens shall be shaken: and then shall appear the sign of the Son of man in heaven: and then shall all the tribes of the earth mourn, and they shall see the Son of man coming in the clouds of heaven with power and great glory. And he shall send his angels with a great sound of a trumpet, and they shall gather together his elect from the four winds, from one end of heaven to the other" (Matt. 24:29–31).

Ezekiel promised the same regathering when he said, "And I will bring you out from the people, and will gather you out of the countries wherein ye are scattered. . . . And I will cause you to pass under the rod, and I will bring you into the bond of the covenant: And I will purge out from among you the rebels, and them that transgress against me: I will bring them forth out of the country where they sojourn, and they shall not enter into the land of Israel: and ye shall know that I am the Lord" (Ezek. 20:34–38).

Amos saw this restoration when he wrote, "And I will bring again the captivity of my people of Israel, and they shall build the waste cities, and inhabit them; and they shall plant vineyards, and drink the wine thereof; they shall also make gardens, and eat the fruit of them. And I will plant them upon their land, and they shall no more be pulled up out of their land which I have given them, saith the Lord thy God" (Amos 9:14–15). He gave the ultimate solution to the Arab-Israeli dispute when he said, "In that day will I raise up the tabernacle of David that is fallen, and close up the breaches thereof; and I will raise up his ruins, and I will build it as in the days of old: That they may possess the remnant of Edom, and of all the heathen, which are called by my name, saith the Lord that doeth this" (Amos 9:11–12). The Arabs are the "remnant of Edom," the descendants of Esau. Amos told us that Israel will eventually occupy the land possessed by the Arab states, which was promised to Israel in Genesis 15.

We might well ask, "What is the relation of the state of Israel to this prophetic program? Have these prophecies already been fulfilled? Will there be a future fulfillment in the establishment of the state of Israel?"

A study of Scripture compels us to say that the establishment of the state of Israel is not the direct fulfillment of these prophecies. God today is not working toward the fulfillment of the program for Israel. That nation was temporarily set aside when they rejected Christ, and God today is calling out from among both Jew and Gentile a people for His name (Acts 15:14). God will not fulfill these prophecies for Israel until the church, His program for this age, is removed. God is setting the stage for this great drama. He is getting the actors in place so He can move at a moment's notice to fulfill His plan. Coming events are casting their shadows ahead of them. The world is being made conscious of Israel because God has never forgotten the promises He made to her in the days of Abraham.

One Saturday night years ago, while driving home from a speaking engagement, my mind was rehearsing the message I planned to preach the next morning on the parable of the fig tree in the Lord's Olivet discourse (Matt. 24 and 25). When I turned on the car radio to listen to the news, I was electrified to hear the announcer say that the United Nations had decided to give Palestine to Israel and to recognize the Jewish state being established there. After I delivered the message, the people were certain I had prepared it *following* the announcement from the United Nations. But the message was timely not because I prepared it after I heard the news but because it proclaimed what God had promised generations ago.

6

Christ's Title Deed
to the Throne

2 Samuel 7:4–17

IN CONSIDERING THE QUESTION of Israel's title deed to Palestine, we find that God added an affirmation to His promise to Abraham concerning the land of Palestine: "And I will make thee exceeding fruitful, and I will make nations of thee, and kings shall come out of thee. And I will establish my covenant between me and thee and thy seed after thee in their generations for an everlasting covenant, to be a God unto thee and to thy seed after thee. And I will give unto thee, and thy seed after thee the land wherein thou art a stranger" (Gen. 17:6–8). Verse 6 contains another significant addition: "kings shall come out of thee."

At creation, God said, "Let us make man in our image, after our likeness: and let them have dominion. . . ." (Gen. 1:26). God outlined the sphere of dominion He gave to Adam. He was to exercise authority over all created things. This earth was subject to the authority of man. To

Adam, the first man and head of the race, God gave the right to reign. Adam was "lord of all he surveyed." From the time of creation, God ruled through the man whom He appointed ruler. Although Adam was never called a king, he manifested all the prerogatives of a king as he reigned over creation.

From the time of the fall until God made a promise to Abraham, authority was centered in the head of the family, or in human government, but there were no rulers called kings. When God said, "Kings shall come out of thee," He was anticipating the means by which He would ultimately rule over all the earth—through a King of His appointment.

When the patriarch Jacob pronounced a prophetic message concerning each of his sons, he said something significant concerning Judah. "Judah, thou art he whom thy brethren shall praise: thy hand shall be in the neck of thine enemies; thy father's children shall bow down before thee" (Gen. 49:8). Here the superiority of Judah over all his brethren is predicted. Jacob continued, "The sceptre shall not depart from Judah, nor a lawgiver from between his feet, until Shiloh come" (Gen. 49:10). Shiloh may be rendered, "He whose right it is," that is, "He whose right it is to rule." This was a prophecy concerning the Messiah, the Lord Jesus Christ, who would come from Judah's line. From this time on, Israel had the right to expect a king.

Until God sent the promised king, He would continue to rule Israel through His appointed representatives. He used patriarchs, such as Moses, the great leader who delivered Israel from Egypt, and Joshua, who brought them out of the wilderness into the promised land. God raised them up to lead the nation and gave them authority over the people, but they were not kings. When they came into Palestine, God raised up judges and gave them His authority to rule, but they were not kings. And yet that promise was always there, "The sceptre shall not depart from Judah."

First Samuel 8:4–6 records a significant event. "Then all the elders of Israel gathered themselves together, and came to Samuel unto Ramah, and said unto him, 'Behold, thou art old, and thy sons walk not in thy ways: now make us a king to judge us like all the nations.' But the thing displeased Samuel, when they said, 'Give us a king to judge us.' And Samuel prayed unto the Lord. And the Lord said unto Samuel, 'Hearken unto the voice of the people in all that they say unto thee: for they have not rejected thee, but they have rejected me, that I should not reign over them.'" Israel wanted a king who would begin a self-perpetuating dynasty.

God responded to their request by permitting them to have Saul as their king. After Saul's death, God appointed David as king in Israel. He had a profitable reign, expanding the boundaries of the land, consolidating the kingdom, and enriching the treasury. In one of the more significant chapters in all the Old Testament, David revealed the desire of his heart. He longed to build a house for the Lord. Nathan the prophet said to him, "Go, do all that is in thine heart, for the Lord is with thee" (2 Sam. 7:3).

God, however, wanted Solomon, the prince of peace, not David, the man of war, to build His temple. But God entered into a covenant contract with David. "And when thy days be fulfilled, and thou shalt sleep with thy fathers, I will set up thy seed after thee, which shall proceed out of thy bowels, and I will establish his kingdom" (2 Sam.

7:12). This made David rejoice. When Saul became king he expected to establish a dynasty that would reign over Israel for generations. But God did not permit Saul's sons to sit on the throne. Instead, He reached out to another tribe, to an obscure family, and took the least son in the family and put him on the throne. God could have done so again after David's death. But God promised David that his throne would always be occupied by one of his sons.

God had even more to promise David. He continued, "And he shall build an house for my name, and I will establish the throne of his kingdom *for ever*" (2 Sam. 7:13). He did not say that David's son Solomon was to reign forever, but that the throne was to be forever occupied by one of David's descendants.

God also revealed the method by which He would deal with David's sons when they sat on the throne. "I will be his father and he shall be my son. If he commit iniquity, I will chasten him with the rod of men, and with the stripes of the children of men: But my mercy shall not depart away from him, as I took it from Saul, whom I put away before thee" (2 Sam. 7:16).

There are three important words in this verse: house, kingdom, and throne. "Thine house" is the Davidic lineage, descendants in David's line who could sit on David's throne. "Thy kingdom" is the kingdom of Israel, the seed of Abraham over which David reigned. "Thy throne" is his royal authority, the right to rule as God's representative. Twice in this one verse God said to David that his dynasty, kingdom, and throne would last *forever*. David responded by saying, "Who am I, O Lord God? and what is my house, that thou hast brought me hitherto? And this was yet a small thing in thy sight, O Lord God; but thou hast spoken also of thy servant's house for a great while to come" (2 Sam. 7:18–19). David recognized that the authority given to his sons was not because of anything in himself. It was a manifestation of God's grace as God moved to fulfill the promise of Genesis 49:10, giving the scepter to David's family until He whose right it is to reign ascends the throne. As yet we have not seen the King reigning; we have not seen Shiloh come. In spite of this, the promise remains that David's son must sit on David's throne to rule over David's kingdom forever.

The gospel of Matthew breaks God's silence of more than four hundred years and gives a message to the nation Israel concerning a King. Matthew wrote, "The book of the generation of Jesus Christ, the son of David, the son of Abraham" (Matt. 1:1). Why single out these two men? Because God gave to these two the great covenant promises that governed God's program for the nation Israel. As the son of Abraham, Christ fulfills God's promise that through Abraham all families of the earth would be blessed. As the son of David, He has the right to rule.

Luke 1 records the announcement of the birth of Jesus Christ to Mary, the woman to whom David's Son was born. The angel addressed Mary, saying, "Fear not, Mary: for thou hast found favour with God. And, behold, thou shalt conceive in thy womb, and bring forth a son, and shall call his name JESUS. He shall be great. . . ." (Luke 1:30–31). There are many areas of greatness. The prophets were great because they announced a message from God. Moses was great because he was the lawgiver. Abraham was great because he was the father of a new nation. In what way would Mary's Son be great?

First, He would be great because of His person. "He
shall be great and shall be called the Son of the Highest"
(v. 32). Second, He would be great because of His work or
office. "The Lord God shall give unto him the throne of
his father David: and he shall reign over the house of
Jacob for ever; and of his kingdom there shall be no end"
(vv. 32–33). The angel used the same three words that
God used in making His covenant with David: throne,
kingdom, and house. The One born to Mary would meet
every requirement to be Israel's Shiloh. At His birth, He
was introduced to the nation Israel as the One in whom
the promises of David would be fulfilled, Shiloh.

When Jesus Christ presented Himself to the nation
Israel at the beginning of His ministry, He took the place
of a teacher or interpreter of the Old Testament. When
He selected the scroll of Isaiah and read a familiar Mes-
sianic portion, His announcement startled the people,
"This day is this scripture fulfilled in your ears" (Luke
4:21). He announced that Shiloh had come. His words and
His works were spoken and performed to prove His claim.
At the close of Christ's earthly life, Pilate said to the
people, "'Behold your King!' But they cried out, 'Away
with him, away with him, crucify him.' Pilate saith unto
them, 'Shall I crucify your King?' The chief priests answered, 'We have no king but Caesar'" (John 19:14–15).
The nation did not reject Jesus Christ because He was
an impostor, was born of the wrong family, came from
the wrong tribe, or could not prove His claims to Messiah-
ship. They rejected Him because they were unwilling to
let Him reign. The superscription over His cross was their
accusation against Him: "Jesus of Nazareth, King of the
Jews."

Nearly two thousand years have passed since Christ came the first time. Concerning Christ's second coming David prophesied: "Let us break their bands asunder and cast away their cords from us" (Ps. 2:1–3). The nations united themselves together in their councils and refused to let Shiloh, David's Son, God's Messiah, rule over them. In spite of the rejection and antagonism of the nations, God the Father said, "Yet have I set my king upon the holy hill of Zion" (v. 6). The Father made a promise to the Son: "Thou art my Son; this day have I begotten thee. Ask of me, and I shall give thee the heathen for thine inheritance, and the uttermost parts of the earth for thy possession" (vv. 7–8). The nations said, "We will not let this one rule over us." Israel said, "We refuse to let this man exercise His reign over us." But the Father said, "Yet have I set my king upon my holy hill of Zion." *Shiloh shall come!*

In Psalm 110 we find the words the Father used to welcome His Son into glory after His death, resurrection, and ascension. During the hours the Son was on the cross the Father turned His face away, causing the Son to cry out, "My God, my God, why hast thou forsaken me?" Because the Son was made sin for us, the Father had to turn from Him. Jesus Christ died spiritually as well as physically so that we who were spiritually dead might be made alive and so that all who died in Christ might receive a glorified body by physical resurrection. After the Resurrection, when the work of redemption had been accomplished, the Father again could turn His face to the Son and receive the Son into His own bosom. On the day of ascension, as the Son came into glory, He heard the Father say, "Sit thou at my right hand, until I make thine enemies thy footstool. The Lord shall send the rod of thy strength out of Zion: rule thou in the midst of thine enemies. Thy people shall be willing in the day of thy power, in the beauties of holiness from the womb of the morning: thou hast the dew of thy youth" (Ps. 110:1–3).

The Son is installed in a priestly ministry until the Father sends Him to earth to reign as King of kings and Lord of lords. He is ministering in the heavenly sanctuary in the presence of God for us now. At the installation of the Son in this ministry, the Father made it clear that the unbelief of the nation Israel did not change His purpose. The Son has not been made a Priest *instead* of a King. The day will come when He will reign over the earth: "Sit thou at my right hand, until I make thine enemies thy footstool."

Revelation 19 gives us a picture of the day when He will return to rule. John wrote, "I saw heaven opened, and behold a white horse." In prophetic Scriptures a white horse symbolizes victory, and a rider on a white horse pictures a victor. John said of this Victor: "He that sat upon him was called Faithful and True, and in righteousness he doth judge and make war. His eyes were as a flame of fire, and on his head were many crowns" (Rev. 19:11–12).

Christ wears a crown because all authority is given to the Son by the Father to reign over all nations. "The kingdoms of this world are become the kingdoms of our Lord, and of his Christ; and he shall reign for ever and ever. And the four and twenty elders, which sat before God on their seats, fell upon their faces, and worshipped God, saying, 'We give thee thanks, O Lord God Almighty, which art, and wast, and art to come; because

thou hast taken to thee thy great power, and hast reigned'"
(Rev. 11:15–17). All things shall be subjected to His authority. Thus at His coming He is seen wearing "many
crowns" to symbolize His absolute authority.

John concluded this portrait of the coming King by
saying, "And he hath on his vesture and on his thigh a
name written, KING OF KINGS, AND LORD OF
LORDS" (Rev. 19:16). He will demonstrate that all
authority is His by bringing all things, including His enemies, into subjection to Himself (Rev. 19:17–21). Thus,
as David's son, He will fulfill the promise God made to
David that his son would reign on his throne.

Matthew shows us a picture of the Lord's return to
reign. "And then shall appear the sign of the Son of man
in heaven: and then shall all the tribes of the earth mourn,
and they shall see the Son of man coming in the clouds of
heaven with power and great glory" (Matt. 24:30). "When
the Son of man shall come in his glory, and all the holy
angels with him, then shall he sit upon the throne of his
glory: And before him shall be gathered all nations. . . ."
(Matt. 25:31). This throne of glory is none other than the
throne of David. And throughout the millennial age and
throughout the endless ages of eternity, the glory of God
will be manifested to the ends of the earth by the King
who sits on David's throne.

When Jesus Christ comes to earth to reign for a thousand years, He will not leave behind His beloved bride. He
will not separate Himself from His body, the church, of
which He is the living Head. He will bring with Him this
body of redeemed ones so that He might be glorified in
the saints and so that they might share His glory. As the
bride of a king shares in the glory, the privileges, and the

honors of her husband's throne, so we will share His glory and honor. This will fulfill His promise, "And if I go and prepare a place for you, I will come again, and receive you unto myself; that where I am there ye may be also" (John 14:3). As He reigns as KING OF KINGS AND LORD OF LORDS FOR EVER AND EVER, we will share His glory.

7

Daniel's Image and the Federated States of Europe

Daniel 2:31–45

WINSTON CHURCHILL, when he retired from the office of prime minister in Great Britain, said he was going to dedicate the rest of his life and whatever strength and talents he had to the formation of the United States of Europe. The threat to the peace and prosperity of the Western world from Russia was so great that he believed a Federated States of Europe was imperative to preserve peace. What Churchill said was imperative is indeed a divine imperative according to the Word of God.

In Daniel's prophecy, we find a revelation concerning Gentile world history. The book of Daniel was written during a significant time. "In the third year of the reign of Jehoiakim king of Judah came Nebuchadnezzar king of Babylon unto Jerusalem, and besieged it" (Dan. 1:1). The citizens of Jerusalem and Palestine were transported out of their land into the land of Babylon and were set up in their own community where they would live for about seventy years.

To those who knew the Scriptures, these events were of great significance. When God called Abraham, He gave him a title deed to the land of Palestine. God said that the land belonged to him and his seed forever. When God raised up David as king over Israel, He entered into a covenant with David, promising him that one of his sons would sit upon the throne, reigning over his people and nation, forever. But then a most surprising thing happened. The nation that had been promised the land was removed from it, and the people who had been promised a king were without a king of their own race. They were in subjection to Gentile leaders.

The Jews wondered, "Why has God thus dealt with us? Why has He taken us out of our land? Why has He taken away our king? Why are we strangers in a strange land with no right of self-government and no self-determination? Will the land of Palestine again become our possession? Will we yet have our own king to reign over us?"

The prophecies of the Old Testament explain why God sent them into Babylon. The prophet Isaiah looked at the condition of the nation and saw their sins, for which there was no covering. The prophet Hosea saw Israel as an unfaithful wife who had gone whoring after idols. The prophet Ezekiel spoke of the departure of the glory of God from the nation because Israel had followed after heathen gods. A righteous God must chasten His children, must discipline them for their disobedience.

The prophet Daniel was in that land of Babylon. Because his heart was burdened with grief for his people, he turned to God to ask, "How is God going to deal with the nation Israel and what is His program for the Gentiles?"

Daniel began his prophecy when Israel was carried out of the land of promise, the place of blessing, into the land of Babylon. Daniel was inquiring on behalf of a chastened people.

The personal history of Daniel and his companions is given in Daniel 1. From chapter 2 we learn about a dream that troubled King Nebuchadnezzar. When he awoke he could no longer recall the dream. Yet he realized it had great significance. He called together all his wise men, astrologers, and soothsayers and charged them to recall his dream and tell him what it meant. When they were unable to do so, Nebuchadnezzar sent them to be executed. Daniel sought clemency for them and asked for time to see if God would reveal the dream to him. Then he went to his house and made the thing known to his companions Hananiah, Mishael, and Azariah, so they too could pray for God's help. Daniel not only laid the thing before God himself, he brought into the prayer meeting other godly Jews who were in the habit of waiting upon God in prayer. As a result, God revealed Nebuchadnezzar's dream, and Daniel was able to tell the king his dream and give him the interpretation of it.

God revealed to Daniel the powers and kingdoms that would reign over Israel and have authority over Palestine and Jerusalem from the time of Daniel until the Messiah reigns over Palestine and the Jews.

Daniel addressed the king: "Thou, O king, sawest, and beheld a great image. This great image, whose brightness was excellent, stood before thee; and the form thereof was terrible" (Dan. 2:31). The image was so overpowering that it dwarfed those standing before it. It was bright, glorious, and awesome. The head was of fine gold, the breast and arms of silver, the belly and thighs of brass, the legs of iron, and the feet of part iron and part clay.

The significant thing to Daniel was that this great image was made up of four different metals, each one harder than the one that went before—gold, the softest; silver, harder; brass, harder yet; and finally iron, the hardest and most indestructible of all. The image was a unit, but Daniel recognized from the four different metals that there were four parts of the image and its meaning. Then Daniel saw a stone smite the feet of the image and break the whole image to pieces (Dan. 2:35).

The stone Daniel saw was a power other than human power that destroyed the image, reduced it to powder dust, scattered it abroad, and then took over the authority of the kingdom represented by the four parts of the great image.

In verses 37–43, we find Daniel's interpretation of this dream. "Thou, O King Nebuchadnezzar, art the head of gold." This meant that Nebuchadnezzar, the head of the Babylonian empire, represented the first world empire that was to rule over the Jews, control the land of Palestine, and have authority over Jerusalem. "After thee shall arise another kingdom, inferior to thee." This second kingdom, the silver breast and arms of verse 32, was the Medo-Persian Empire, for the Medes conquered the Babylonians and then united with the Persians to form a second great world empire. "Another third kingdom of brass which shall bear rule over all the earth." We know from history that Alexander was victorious over the Medo-Persian coalition and that Alexander's Greek Empire then ruled over the territory previously held by the Babylonians and the Medo-Persians. Verse 40 describes the fourth kingdom as being "as strong as iron." This was the Roman Empire, which overthrew the Greek Empire and ruled over all the territory that the Greeks had held. So Daniel was giving to us, in the interpretation of this vision, the succession of four world empires that would reign over the Jews and Palestine.

Daniel showed only a slight interest in the first three empires. He gave little more than a sentence to the Babylonians, the Medo-Persians, and the Greeks (vv. 38–39). Daniel was most concerned with the fourth world empire (vv. 40–43), the Roman Empire, which would be as strong as iron. Whereas the Babylonians had exerted influence, the Medo-Persians a greater influence, and the Greeks a yet greater influence, Rome exerted the most powerful and dominating influence of any empire in history. It was truly an iron kingdom and Rome ruled with an iron fist, as expressed in verse 40: "Breaketh in pieces and subdueth all things: and as iron that breaketh all these, shall it break in pieces and bruise." Every part of the former three kingdoms was brought under the influence of Rome. Every portion of the land that had belonged to Babylon, Medo-Persia, and Greece was gripped in the iron fist of the Roman Empire. But as we study this image we notice that the Roman Empire becomes weak. The feet and toes were made of iron and *clay*. The kingdom was divided. As the Roman Empire progressed, its authority was weakened by being divided into separate parts. The toes of the feet were "part of iron and part of clay so that the kingdom shall be partly strong and partly broken," or partly divided. The longer the Roman Empire existed, the weaker it would become, until finally, when it got down to the toes, the last form of the Gentile world power, it would be divided into ten toes, or ten kingdoms.

When an empire is divided into many parts the inevitable result is weakness. Why was Rome strong in its beginning? Because it held all things together with its iron fist. But with the division came progressive weakening.

Chapter 2 revealed the progress of Gentile world empires from a human standpoint, through the eyes of Nebuchadnezzar. When he looked at world power he saw something splendid and awesome, something to be feared, revered, and honored.

In chapter 7, Daniel had a vision of his own. This one revealed the same course of Gentile world power but from the divine standpoint. Instead of an awesome image, Daniel saw four monstrous beasts. He watched as "the four winds of heaven strove upon the great sea. And four great beasts came up from the sea, diverse one from another" (Dan. 7:3). When the sea is mentioned in prophecy it symbolizes Gentile nations. "The wicked are like the troubled sea, when it cannot rest, whose waters cast up mire and dirt. There is no peace, saith my God, to the wicked" (Isa. 57:20–21). When God referred to Gentile nations in their rebellion against Him, their hatred of Him, and their godlessness, He pictured them as the restless, wind-tossed sea.

Daniel saw four beasts arise out of this sea of Gentile nations. The first one was like a lion and had eagle's wings. That sounds like a rather strange-looking beast, but it was the national symbol of Babylon. The first beast was the head of gold of the image in chapter 2—Babylonia. The second beast was "like to a bear, and it raised up itself on one side." This is a picture of the Medo-Persian coalition; the Persians became the dominant nation and they ruled over the Medes. The three ribs in its mouth, I believe, are the Babylonian Empire, the Median Empire, and the Persian Empire, all of which were brought together under this one dominating head. This second beast, the lopsided bear, paralleled the silver shoulders and arms of the image of Daniel 2. Then a third beast arose that looked "like a leopard, which had upon the back of it four wings of a fowl," and it had four heads. The leopard was known for its speed, and this was God's way of picturing the speed of Alexander's conquest, which in just a few short months swept over all of the world and swallowed up the Medo-Persian Empire. It had wings of a fowl so that it could move rapidly. It had four heads, representing the four great generals under Alexander, among whom the kingdom was divided after Alexander's death. This third beast corresponds with the belly and thigh of brass of chapter 2.

In verse 7, Daniel described the fourth beast. It was "dreadful and terrible, and strong exceedingly; and it had great iron teeth: it devoured and brake in pieces, and stamped the residue with the feet of it: and it was diverse from all the beasts that were before it; and it had ten horns" (v. 7). Daniel does not liken it to a lion, bear, or any other animal. It is a composite of all the beasts that went before it, which it swallowed.

The significant thing about this beast is that it has ten horns (Dan. 7:24). A horn in prophetic Scripture symbolizes a king. Thus Daniel saw ten kingdoms as the final form of this empire. We see the same picture in chapter 2, where Daniel said that the last form of Gentile power would be the ten-toed state that had been divided and made weak. The ten horns of 7:7 correspond to the ten toes of 2:42. After the fall of Rome, the authority of the old Roman Empire moved to the north, and the center of power moved from place to place in Europe. There was division and further division until the Middle Ages, when kingdom divided against kingdom, warring against another kingdom that had originally been a part of the old Roman Empire.

Looking at Europe today, we see continued division of the old Roman Empire. A great problem facing Western powers today is how to bring together nations that were originally part of the same empire. France won't get together with Germany, and Germany won't get together with Britain, and so it goes. Europe today is in the condition Daniel saw in his vision—no unifying factor; the power that once resided in the fist of Rome has been spread among many nations.

John saw the same thing in his vision, which is recorded in the book of Revelation: "I stood upon the sand of the sea, and I saw a beast rise up out of the sea" (13:1). This sounds like Daniel 7, where Daniel wrote about seeing beasts come out of the sea. The beast John saw had seven heads and ten horns. It was "like a leopard, and his feet were as the feet of a bear, and his mouth as the mouth of a lion" (v. 2). Those were the same three beasts that we read about in Daniel 7. John and Daniel were talking about the same thing.

John added to what Daniel revealed. He described in detail the last ruler of the Gentile world powers. "The beast that thou sawest was, and is not; and shall ascend out of the bottomless pit" (Rev. 17:8). After having great authority, its authority was destroyed, but it is going to have its old authority again: "They beheld the beast that was, and is not, and yet is." The power of Rome, dissipated through division, became weak, impotent, and help-less. But it will become powerful and world-dominating again.

John explained, "The ten horns which thou sawest are ten kings. And they have not received their kingdoms as yet, but they receive power as kings one hour with this beast" (v. 12). These ten kings that head the nations in the last stage of Gentile world power "have one mind, and shall give their power and strength unto this beast" (v. 13). John indicated that from the time Rome conquered Greece, Palestine would be under the control of some power that had been part of the old Roman Empire. Although the Roman Empire would become weak through division and subdivision, Palestine would still be controlled by some nation that had been part of it. After World War I, the right to rule Palestine passed from the Turks to the British Empire, a part of the old Roman Empire. The historic land of Palestine has never been ruled by any power outside the Roman Empire from the time of the Roman conquest until the present.

According to Revelation 13 and 17, the nations that once were a part of the Roman Empire will eventually agree to give their authority to one man as their head. My studies of the prophetic Scripture have led me to conclude that Russia will become so strong and powerful that the nations that once comprised the Roman Empire will be forced to unite. They will say, "We have no defense against the power of the 'king of the North,' Russia, unless we unite. We must forget our national boundaries and give up some of our own sovereign rights to protect ourselves from Russia." And so these nations, in their divided state, will become single-minded and give authority to the Beast.

This new Roman Empire, or the Federated States of Europe, will not come into existence because one nation becomes powerful and conquers the rest of Europe; the federation will be by mutual consent. The Beast will be a world dictator who will rule with all of the authority and the iron power that ancient Rome once exercised.

I believe we are living in the most significant of days. The Roman power has divided and subdivided until it has become weak. The rise of the king of the North threatens the peace and security of the world. The countries of Europe are crying for defense against this Russian power. The only solution is unification. How long it will take them to unite I do not know, but with world conditions in such a shambles I don't think it would take much of a threat to drive France, Germany, Spain, Italy, Great Britain, the rest of the Roman world, and the United States into a mutual defense pact.

Daniel told us that a smiter will terminate Gentile world power (2:34–35). He spoke of "the days of these kings" (2:44), referring to the days of the ten toes, when the divided nations of Europe will again be united. In those days shall "the God of heaven set up a kingdom, which shall never be destroyed. . . . Forasmuch as thou sawest that the stone was cut out of the mountain without hands, and that it brake in pieces the iron, the brass, the clay, the silver, and the gold; the great God hath made known to the king what shall come to pass hereafter" (v. 44–45).

The thrones Daniel mentioned in 7:9 were the thrones of the ten horns, the ten toes, or the ten kingdoms. When that comes to pass "the Ancient of Days" will sit, Daniel said. The Ancient of Days is the Lord Jesus Christ, who has the right to reign. "his garments were white as snow and the hair of his head like the pure wool: his throne was like the fiery flame, and his wheels as burning fire. A fiery stream issued and came forth from before him: thousand thousands ministered unto him, and ten thousand times ten thousand stood before him: the judgment was set" (7:9–10). This is a picture of the Son of God coming to destroy the coalition of nations so that Jesus Christ himself might reign.

In Revelation 11:15 John transported us to the Second Coming of Christ when he wrote, "And the seventh angel sounded; and there were great voices in heaven, saying, 'The kingdoms of this world are become the kingdom of our Lord and of his Christ; and he shall reign for ever and ever.'"

8

The Coming World Dictator

Revelation 13:1–10

THE WORLD IS HEADED TOWARD a unified political and religious system that defies imagination. The Word of God has much to say about the warfare between God and Satan, between this world and the heavenlies. Scriptures reveal that this conflict will climax when Satan brings his masterpiece, the man of sin, the Beast, on the world scene as head of a confederation of nations. The coming worldwide dictatorship will center on the worship of Satan and will be characterized by lawlessness, godlessness, and authoritarianism. The dictator will aim to exterminate every believer in Jesus Christ and to outlaw God from the universe.

Daniel wrote that he saw in the night visions "a fourth beast, dreadful and terrible, and strong exceedingly; and it had great iron teeth: it devoured and brake in pieces, and stamped the residue with the feet of it" (7:7). Daniel described a great conquering power that subjugated all things to itself. "It was diverse from all other beasts that were before it," he said. The thing about the beast that stood out in Daniel's mind was its ten horns. This was no natural beast; it was a monstrosity, having grown beyond its intended size and shape, just as the Gentile world will grow and encompass the earth.

Daniel then described these horns: "I considered the horns, and, behold, there came up among them another little horn" (v. 8). He saw a little horn, the eleventh, beginning to arise. As he watched it grow, he saw that it plucked out three other horns by the roots. This horn, in coming to a place of prominence, put down some existing world power or military might. The horn had "eyes like the eyes of a man," which symbolize its great intelligence or wisdom, and a "mouth speaking great things," which stresses its authority.

This passage and others indicate that this individual will be known for his big mouth. He will be a blasphemer and a dictator. Daniel may well have wondered what this vision meant. Fortunately, we are not left to human speculation; God also gave the interpretation to Daniel. Verse 17 explains. These four beasts are four kings that will arise out of the earth, the four great world powers. The fourth beast particularly intrigued Daniel. It was different from the others. "The fourth beast shall be the fourth kingdom upon earth [what we know as the Roman Empire, the fourth of the four great beasts that controlled Palestine and ruled over Jerusalem], which shall be diverse from all kingdoms, and shall devour the whole earth" (v. 23).

In its early form the Roman Empire never occupied the whole earth. It controlled the Mediterranean world, dominated the European sector, and had authority in North

Africa, but it did not occupy the whole earth. Daniel revealed that this fourth beast, before it is put to death, will devour the whole earth.

Verse 24 explains some of the details. The ten horns of this kingdom are ten kings that will arise. Another king will arise after them and be diverse from the first. This shows us that these horns represent ten men with their ten kingdoms. The little horn that Daniel saw represents a man who will consolidate the territory ruled over by the other ten.

Verse 25 mentions his mouth again. "He shall speak great words against the most High." The Most High is Jehovah, the God of Israel, the Almighty one. This man is not raving against other kings to persuade them to come into his camp. He is speaking against Almighty God, challenging God's right to reign over the universe. Not only will he speak against the Most High, but he "shall wear out the saints of the most High." The saints of the Most High are Daniel's own people, his own nation, his own city, and his own land. The saints of the Most High are also believers among the nation Israel who will come to know the Lord during the tribulation. During this period 144,000 Jews will be converted the same way the apostle Paul was converted on the Damascus road (Rev. 7). God will suddenly remove their blindness, they will recognize Christ as Messiah, and they will "look on him whom they have pierced." They are the saints of the Most High who have a worldwide ministry to bring the knowledge of Christ to every nation.

The new world ruler will show special antagonism toward the Most High and His saints, and he will try "to change times and laws." He will reject all laws previously instituted and will set in place his own lawless system. Because of this, we refer to him as "the lawless one" (2 Thess. 2:3). Israel, the saints of God, "shall be given into his hands until a time and times and the dividing of time," or three and one-half years. This individual will have worldwide authority for the last three and one-half years of the seven-year tribulation.

The key to understanding Daniel 7–12 is knowing that Daniel's focus is on this final world ruler and his kingdom. Some of the events Daniel referred to have since been fulfilled on one level, but they also foreshadow the final form of Gentile world power and its ruler. In chapter 8 Daniel described a king who would conquer the Medo-Persian Empire, an event that took place several centuries after Daniel lived. Antiochus Epiphanes came out of the Grecian Empire, a great enemy of Israel. He showed his contempt for the Jews and their religion by slaughtering a pig in the temple in Jerusalem and putting its blood on the altar. He was known as "the desolator." This passage refers not only to Antiochus but also to the great desolator to come, the one called "the little horn" in Daniel 7.

We read of this one and his work in Daniel 8:23. He appears "in the latter time of their kingdom." The "latter time" or the "last time" almost always refers to the tribulation period. He said, "In the latter times of their kingdom, when the transgressors are come to the full, a king of fierce countenance, understanding dark sentences, shall stand up. And his power shall be mighty, but not by his own power." He will get his power from a source outside himself. According to Revelation 17:13, he will get it from other nations who consent to give him authority. But according to Revelation 13:2, he will get it from Satan.

Daniel continued his description, saying, "he shall destroy wonderfully," and he "shall prosper, and practice, and shall destroy the mighty and the holy people. And through his policy also he shall cause craft to prosper in his hand; and he shall magnify himself in his heart, and by peace shall destroy many" (Dan. 8:24–25). By guaranteeing the Jews that he will give them the land of Palestine, he convinces them that he is their God. "He shall stand up against the Prince of princes" (v. 25). The Prince of princes is the Lord Jesus Christ Himself, for Isaiah 9:6 calls Christ the Prince of Peace. "But he shall be broken without hand" (v. 25). God will move in to destroy this individual.

In Daniel 9:24, Daniel wrote about the coming Messiah and the work He will do. He will finish the transgression, make an end of sin, and make reconciliation for iniquity. Then He will bring in everlasting righteousness, seal up the vision and prophecy, and anoint the most holy place, or the Most Holy One. His work will fulfill all that God promised Israel. But Messiah will be rejected at His coming, as prophesied in verse 26, where Daniel said that Messiah shall be cut off.

The destruction of Jerusalem is God's punishment upon Israel for rejecting Christ. This prophecy refers to the destruction of Jerusalem that took place under Titus in the year 70 A.D. This destruction was by "the people of the prince that shall come." The "*prince* that shall come" is a Roman prince and the "*people* of the prince that shall come" are the Romans. So Daniel was revealing that Romans would destroy the city of Jerusalem and the temple.

Daniel said this prince (i.e., the "little horn," or "the king of fierce countenance") "shall confirm the covenant with many for one week" (v. 27), that is, for seven years. When this world ruler comes to authority in the European federation of nations he will see that the Arab-Israeli dispute threatens world peace. He will make a covenant with the Jews, guaranteeing their independence in the land of Palestine, and he will give Palestine to them. The nation will conclude that he who gives Palestine back to them must be the one of whom Abraham spoke. They will be convinced that he has fulfilled the Abrahamic covenant and will acknowledge him as God and Messiah. But he will break this covenant and move into Palestine and set up a false religious system. Revelation 13:11–18 further describes this abomination of desolation.

His Person

In chapter 11, Daniel had more to say about this person. He was called the "little horn" in chapter 7, the "king of fierce countenance" in chapter 8, and the "prince that shall come" in chapter 9. In chapter 11 Daniel called him the king that "shall do according to his own will" (v. 16), or as we sometimes refer to him, "the willful king." This passage shows his authority over Palestine. Daniel said he "shall do according to his will; he shall exalt himself, and magnify himself above every god, and shall speak marvelous things against the God of gods [there is his mouth again], and shall prosper till the indignation be accomplished" (11:36). The "indignation" is another word for the tribulation period.

According to verse 37 he will not regard the God of his fathers. He will recognize no religion other than the worship of himself and Satan. He will not regard the desire of women. This has been variously interpreted. Some believe the desire of women is the Lord Jesus Christ. Others believe it has to do with the desire of women for rest from war so that their sons can return home. Either is possible in the context. It emphasizes his absolute control and total disregard for right, justice, or the feelings of men or women. He will not regard any God but himself.

He will not only speak against God and prevent any law from operating that would curtail his activity, but he will also set himself up as the object of worship. "He shall magnify himself above all. But in his estate shall he honor the God of forces" (vv. 37–38). In other words, he will honor the God of might. Military power is the only power he will recognize.

We know Daniel's prophecies were a divine revelation because the Lord Jesus put His approval upon all that Daniel spoke. He said, "When ye therefore shall see the abomination of desolation, spoken of by Daniel the prophet, stand in the holy place, (whoso readeth let him understand:) then let them that be in Judea flee to the mountains. . . ." (Matt. 24:15). Christ continued in verse 21, "Then shall be great tribulation such as was not from the beginning of this world to this time, no, nor ever shall be. And except those days should be shortened [or, it would be better to read it, "unless those days should be terminated and brought to an end"], there should no flesh be saved."

This dictator will so dominate and control the world that if God did not bring an end to his corrupt government, he would destroy mankind from the face of the earth. As graphic as Daniel's description was, he was able to reveal only a small portion of what things will be like when this one comes into authority.

The apostle Paul added to this line of teaching in 2 Thessalonians 2. As mentioned before, the Thessalonians were being persecuted, and someone came up with the idea that they were in the tribulation. They concluded that Paul had been wrong in his teaching that the church would be translated before the tribulation began. And so Paul had to write, "We beseech you, brethren, by the coming of our Lord Jesus Christ, and by our gathering together unto him [the rapture], that ye be not soon shaken in mind, or be troubled, neither by spirit, nor by word, nor by letter as from us, as that the day of Christ [or, of the Lord] is at hand" (2 Thess. 2:1).

Evidently someone had produced a false epistle teaching that the day of the Lord had already come. Paul repudiated that as contrary to what he had taught. He proved to them that they could not yet be in the tribulation period by reminding them that the "little horn" of Daniel 7, the "king of fierce countenance" of Daniel 8, the Roman "prince" of Daniel 9, the "willful king" of Daniel 11, and the "abomination that desolates" of Matthew 24 had not yet come. The sure sign that the tribulation period, or the day of the Lord, has begun, Paul said, is that the head of the Federated States of Europe will have appeared and given Israel a covenant to settle the Arab-Israeli dispute. Paul might have added that as long as the Jews are not back in Palestine, this man has not come, and as long as the Federated States of Europe have not combined to give their power to one head, the tribulation period has not begun.

Paul said, "Let no man deceive you [make you believe that we are already in the tribulation period] by any means: for that day shall not come, except there come a falling away first" (v. 3). That falling away may be either a falling away from the faith or the departure he talked about in verse 1, the departure of the saints to be with the Lord. He told them not to be worried, for until this departure took place, and "that man of sin be revealed, the son of perdition," they could not be in the day of the Lord.

The Bible uses many names to reveal facets of this man's character. The apostle Paul referred to him by a new name; he called him "that man of sin, the son of perdition." The use of the word *that* in the phrase "that man of sin" emphasizes that the person is well known.

This "man of sin" is also called "the lawless one" because he will repudiate religion, law, and moral order and replace them with his own aims for world conquest. Anything that promotes his dictatorship he will deem to be right.

He is also called "the son of perdition," which refers to his ruler, Satan himself. He is Satan's chief son. God, to redeem the world, gave His Son. And Satan, to bring all the world under his authority, sends his son—not the son of heaven, not the son of glory, but the son of perdition.

His Work

Again we find his mouth going. "Who opposeth and exalteth himself above all that is called God, or that is worshipped; so that he as God sitteth in the temple of God, showing himself that he is God" (v. 4). This man will set himself up, not only as authority over all the world in a political sense, but also as the head of the world religion; he will make himself the object of worship. He will bring all things, both political and religious, under his authority.

In Revelation 13, John, in essence, repeated Daniel 7 as he described the fourth beast. John did not refer to the first three beasts because they had already passed off the world scene. John lived under the authority of the fourth beast, the Roman Empire. John saw this Beast rise up out of the sea. "The sea" in Revelation symbolizes the Gentile nations. The one who rises up out of the Gentile nations has "seven heads and ten horns, and upon his horns ten crowns, and upon his heads the name of blasphemy" (Rev. 13:1). This is another reference to his mouth. What characterizes this Beast above all else is his pretentious claim, so that he is called "the blasphemer."

Verse 2 reveals that the dragon gave him his power, his throne, and his great authority. And from Revelation 12 we know that the dragon is Satan. So John answered the question, "Where does this man get power that extends its authority to the whole earth?" He gets it from Satan. Satan is formulating one colossal world system to subjugate the whole earth to himself. According to verse 4 the world worships the dragon which gave power to the Beast.

Some people in our day worship Satan. A religious system that has grown up in France, particularly in Paris, says that there is no God besides Satan. This is a precursor of the final world system that will worship Satan. This ruler is called "the Beast" because he will subjugate himself to Satanic control so that he is no more responsible for his actions than a wild beast is for his.

"There was given unto him a mouth [there it is again] speaking great things and blasphemy, and power was given unto him to continue forty and two months" (v. 5). He will exercise his authority over the world for three and one-half years as absolute dictator in political affairs and as god in religious affairs.

"And he opened his mouth in blasphemy against God, to blaspheme his name, and his tabernacle, and them that dwell in heaven" (v. 6). "Them that dwell in heaven" may refer to the saints who have been caught up to meet the Lord in the air, but I think it is Satan's challenge to all the angelic beings. These created angels had an opportunity to follow Satan at the first rebellion and they refused. Near the end he will say to them, "You had your chance to follow me and look where you'd be now if you had. You would be my ministering angels in carrying out this great worldwide system. But where are you now? You are attached to a lost cause."

But Satan himself is deceived. He thinks his power and authority is of his own making, but that is not the case. Authority over the world still belongs to God. According to verse 7, "It was given unto him [Satan] to make war with the saints." All this will happen, not according to Satan's plan and purpose, but as God permits people to demonstrate the wickedness, godlessness, and corruption of the human heart. What appears to be Satan's victory is actually God's way of showing people just how far down the pathway of lawlessness Satan will take them if they follow him. "Power was given him over all kindreds, and tongues, and nations. And all that dwell upon the earth shall worship him, whose names are not written in the book of life of the Lamb slain from the foundation of the world" (13:7–8).

"He that leadeth into captivity shall go into captivity: he that killeth with the sword must be killed with the sword" (v. 10). When this one sits on his throne of authority, the great majority of those who accept Jesus Christ as Savior will be martyred for their faith. His hatred and bitterness toward God will let no one name the name of Christ without being put to death.

In Revelation 19, John reveals the conclusion of Armageddon, the scene of great carnage where armies give the earth a bloodbath unlike any other in history. He said that the Lord Jesus Christ will come from heaven to this earth as a rider on a white horse, whose name is King of kings and Lord of lords. When Jesus Christ comes to earth the second time, the beast will be taken, "and with him the false prophet that wrought miracles before him, with which he deceived them that had received the mark of the beast, and them that worshipped his image. These both were cast alive into a lake of fire burning with brimstone" (v. 20).

When God is ready to send His Son to reign on David's throne, this "beast," this "little horn," this "lawless one," will see the sign of His coming in heaven and will issue an edict, saying, "I forbid God to send His Son Jesus Christ into this earth to reign." God will sit on His throne in heaven and chuckle. "He that sits in the heavens shall laugh" (Ps. 2:4). God will demonstrate that He *is God* by sending His Son to earth and throwing this blasphemous idolater into the lake of fire and judging him with eternal death.

God is still on the throne.

It does not take an astute student to see that we are moving toward these things in our day. The nations of Europe are looking to the North with skepticism and fear, saying, "Our only hope is to unite." Russian Communism and influences such as "glasnost" are driving nations who have been separated for centuries into union. The North Atlantic Treaty Organization and the European Common Market are only portents of the movement. The European states are moving closer toward economic and political federation. The time will come when the nations of Europe will say to one man, "You take authority over us." This man will appear as a savior and deliverer. He will bring peace to the world by settling the Arab-Israeli dispute. But when the influence of Russian Communism lessens and is ultimately wiped out by a judgment of God, the Beast will assume the dictatorship of the world, and no individual will be allowed to buy as much as a loaf of bread or a pint of milk without his permission. Only by submitting to the authority of the Beast will anyone survive.

The United States, as such, is not mentioned in prophecy, but I believe the Federated States of Europe will include the nations born out of Europe. The United States—by its language, system of law, customs, and people—is only an extension of the old Roman Empire's sphere of influence and authority. I am not dogmatic about this, but I understand from my knowledge of Scripture that the United States will be a part of this great system of the Beast.

Some will wonder who the Beast is and whether or not he is alive today. I do not have the faintest idea. People have tried to identify him in the past. Some have believed that Napoleon, Mussolini, Hitler, Stalin, or Khrushchev were the Beast. But Scripture does not identify him, nor does it give us any clue as to when he will arrive, because he will not be revealed to the world until *after* the church is gone. It could be someone who is an international leader, whose true nature and character is not suspected, one to whom all the world will look as a deliverer and never dream that he will give himself to the control of Satan. And it will not be until the church has been translated, until you and I have seen our Lord face to face, that this world will be united under his political and religious authority.

9

The Lamb That Speaks
Like a Dragon

Revelation 13:11–18

THE LATE BELGIAN statesman P. H. Spaak was quoted in the newspaper *LaSeur* as saying, "The truth is that the method of international committees has failed. What we need is a person, someone of the highest order or great experience, of great authority, of wide influence, of great energy. Let him come and let him come quickly. Either a civilian or a military man, no matter what his nationality, who will cut all the red tape, shove out of the way all the committees, wake up all the people and galvanize all governments into action. Let him come quickly. This man we need and for whom we wait will take charge of the defense of the West. Once more I say, it is not too late, but it is high time."

His was another voice pleading for someone to unite the European nations and thereby ward off Communism. What these people do not realize is that when this person comes, he will not only bring nations together under his power, but he will institute a dictatorial reign such as this world has never seen.

A trinity from hell, imitating the holy trinity, will dominate the world scene in the last days before Christ returns to reign. Satan will imitate the work of God the Father; the Beast will imitate the work of the Son by subjecting the world to himself; and the False Prophet will imitate the work of the Holy Spirit by magnifying the false king.

The False Prophet (Rev. 19) is also called "the Second Beast" or "the beast out of the earth" (Rev. 13). Immediately after John saw the beast that arose out of the sea, he said, "And I beheld another beast coming up out of the earth" (13:11). As previously mentioned, the sea symbolizes the Gentile nations. Thus this first Beast of Revelation 13 is the Gentile political ruler. References to land or earth in prophetic Scriptures symbolize the land of Palestine, that portion of the earth given by God to His chosen people, the Israelites. Thus John revealed that a second individual will arise out of the land of Palestine. This person is not a Gentile, as was his predecessor; he is a physical descendant of Abraham, a Jew according to the flesh, who is prominent in the religious sphere. This individual coming up out of the land "had two horns like a lamb, and he spake as a dragon" (v. 11).

When John the Baptist identified the Lord Jesus at the beginning of His ministry, he pointed to the Lord and said, "Behold the Lamb of God, that taketh away the sin of the world." After the fall of man, God instituted the principle that people could approach Him only through blood sacrifices, and He set apart the lamb as the peculiar animal for sacrifice. So when the Lord Jesus Christ came to be the sacrifice for the sins of the world, He came as THE Lamb of God.

Satan, the great imitator and deceiver, will introduce his masterpiece of religious deception as a lamb. But Satan will be unable to say of him, "Behold the lamb that taketh away the sin of the world," for he will not come to bring revelation from God nor salvation. He will bring blindness, lest the light of the glorious Gospel would shine upon them and they would be saved. He will come according to the working of a lie: "Then shall that Wicked be revealed, whom the Lord shall consume with the spirit of his mouth, and shall destroy with the brightness of his coming: Even him, whose coming is after the working of Satan with all power and signs and lying wonders. And with all deceivableness of unrighteousness in them that perish; because they received not the love of the truth, that they might be saved. And for this cause God shall send them strong delusion, that they should believe a lie" (2 Thess. 2:8).

In Genesis, where Satan introduced sin, he did so with a lie, a deliberate and willful deception, a denial of the truth of God. For that reason Jesus called Satan a liar and the father of lies (John 8:44). Satan spoke the world's first lie when he said to Eve, "Ye shall not surely die: For God doth know that in the day ye eat thereof, then your eyes shall be opened, and ye shall be as gods, knowing good and evil" (Gen. 1:4–5). Satan's purpose is to continue to deceive people, to lead them to believe that they can work for their own salvation, to persuade them that their own righteousness will make them acceptable to God.

The False Prophet, or the second beast, will come as a great religious leader. He will offer a balm for the hearts of those burdened and distressed by tribulation, yet he will speak as a dragon; nothing he says will conform to the truth of God nor to Him who is the Way, the Truth, and the Life. It will conform to the one who gives him power and authority, Satan himself.

The authority behind both these beasts is revealed in verse 12: "He exerciseth all the power of the first beast before him." Both are brought to their position in world affairs by Satan. Some think this passage means that the second beast, the religious leader, will do away with the first Beast so that only one beast is in authority during the last half of the tribulation. However, Revelation 19 tells us that Christ will bring judgment upon the first Beast and the False Prophet when He returns to judge and reign. This shows that these two coexist and reign at the same time. The two are so united in their aims, methods, and authority as to be one.

"He exerciseth the power of the first beast before him" means that he gets his authority from Satan. "The dragon gave him his power, and his seat [throne] and great authority" (13:2). The dragon is "that old serpent, called the Devil, and Satan, which deceiveth the whole world," identified for us in Revelation 12:9. This political ruler gets his authority to rule from the dragon, that is, from Satan, who will bring him to the world as his masterpiece of deception. It will be as though Satan is saying to the world, "You have been looking for a king? I will produce a king who will reign over this world and will subject all things to himself. You have been looking for a great religious leader? I will produce a religious leader who will give you one world religion." This is the way Satan will imitate the purpose and program of God.

Revelation 13:12 describes the work of this great religious authority. He "causeth the earth and them that dwell therein to worship the first beast, whose deadly wound was healed." The False Prophet will not try to promote himself; he never becomes an object of worship. His work is to direct attention away from himself to the one who says he has the right to be worshiped. This does not mean that believers brought to Christ by the preaching of the Gospel will worship this Beast. But he will cause "all those who have citizenship in this earth" to worship the Beast. Verse 13 tells us how he will convince people to worship this political world ruler: "He doeth great wonders, so that he maketh fire come down from heaven to the earth in the sight of men, and deceiveth them that dwell on the face of the earth by means of those miracles which he has the power to do in the sight of the beast."

In 2 Kings 1 is an interesting cross reference to this. There we learn that Elijah was authenticated to the nation Israel by the signs and miracles he did. "Elijah answered and said to the captain of fifty, 'If I be a man of God, then let fire come down from heaven, and consume thee and thy fifty.' And there came down fire from heaven, and consumed him and his fifty" (2 Kings 1:10). Further into this chapter we learn that this happened again and again. Elijah was authenticated to the nation Israel by the fire that came from heaven.

The last two verses in the Old Testament say, "Behold, I will send you Elijah the prophet before the coming of the great and dreadful day of the Lord: And he shall turn the heart of the fathers to the children, and the heart of the children to their fathers, lest I come and smite the earth with a curse" (Mal. 4:5–6). In His last spoken words before

a four-hundred-year period of silence, God promised that
Elijah would come before the Lord comes.

When the False Prophet calls down fire from heaven, as
recorded in Revelation 13:13, he does so to add to his
deception. The devil knows the Scriptures. And his representatives know the prophecy of the Bible. They know
that God authenticated His prophet and His messenger
with fire from heaven. So Satan will imitate the miracles of
Elijah through this False Prophet to convince the nation
Israel that the man of sin, the willful king, is the Messiah.

When the second beast works these miracles, a message
goes with them. The Lord Jesus never worked a miracle
just to be spectacular. There was a lesson in every miracle
He performed. The miracle was incidental to the message.
And here we find that these spectacular, satanic miracles
are incidental to the message of the False Prophet: "Saying
to them that dwell on the earth, that they should make an
image to the beast, which had a wound by a sword, and
did live" (v. 14). Satan will cause the False Prophet to set
up a great image in Jerusalem and thus make Jerusalem
the center of a worldwide religion. This shows again the
satanic imitation of God's program. When Christ reigns
on this earth Jerusalem will be His capital city, the center
of a worldwide religious system that recognizes the Son of
God as Deliverer, Savior, and King.

But Satan will set up his own religious system in Jerusalem before Christ returns to reign. Jesus referred to this
scene when He said, "When ye therefore shall see the
abomination of desolation, spoken of by Daniel the
prophet, stand in the holy place, then let them which be in
Judea flee to the mountains" (Matt. 24:15). Then He added,
"There shall arise false Christs, and false prophets, and shall

show great signs and wonders; insomuch that if it were possible, they shall deceive the very elect" (v. 24). In Matthew 24:15–16 Jesus described the setting up of this image, which John later recorded in Revelation 13:14.

This enables us to identify the time period when this False Prophet will come on the world scene. As discussed earlier, the Beast, or the head of the Federated States of Europe, will appear at the beginning of the tribulation, seven years before Christ returns to earth to reign. His true character will not be revealed for three and one-half years, the middle of the tribulation, when Satan will move in and cause the False Prophet to set up a great image in Jerusalem and proclaim that all the world must worship it. In worshiping this image, they are worshiping the head of the Federated States of Europe.

The ministry of the False Prophet is further described in verse 14: "Saying to them that dwell on the earth, that they should make an image to the beast, which had the wound by the sword, and did live. And he had power to give life unto the image of the beast, that the image of the beast should both speak, and cause that as many as would not worship the image of the beast should be killed." I don't profess to know how the False Prophet will make this image speak—whether he will do it electronically, by ventriloquism, or by some satanic marvel. But I know this is something so awesome that the world, when it hears this dead and lifeless image give commands, will fall down before it as though it had come from Almighty God Himself, as though that world ruler were the Messiah sent from God and this False Prophet was his high priest.

Not only does the False Prophet have power to give life to the Beast, but he also has the power of life and death over every individual in the Federated States of Europe, the kingdom of the Beast. He has power to "cause that as many as would not worship the image of the beast should be killed" (v. 15). Verse 7 says, "It was given unto him to make war with the saints, and to overcome them." It does not say what method he will use to overcome the saints, but it does tell us how he will move against all who have accepted Christ as Savior. He will set up a religious system with himself as god and this apostate Jew as False Prophet, and he will try to make every individual in the world accept a sign of subjection to his authority. "He causeth all, both small and great, rich and poor, free and bond, to receive a mark in their right hand, or in their foreheads: and that no man might buy or sell, save he that had the mark, or the name of the beast, or the number of his name" (v. 16). Without this identifying sign—this mark of submission to his authority and acknowledgment of his deity—no individual will be able to buy or sell. Whoever refuses to submit to the authority of this system will either starve to death or be slain by the government, who will treat as traitors all who refuse to accept the identifying mark.

This worldwide system, so intricately planned and so devilishly manipulated, will control every item of commerce. That is why John, in Revelation 7, saw multitudes from every tribe and nation who have been martyred for their faith. They are the ones who would not submit to the authority of this system because of their personal faith in the Lord Jesus Christ. As a result, they are slain.

Verse 18 is a puzzling one: "Let him that hath understanding count the number of the beast: for it is the number of a man; and his number is six hundred three score and six." I confess that I don't know what this number means. I am certain, however, that there are more than 666 interpretations. Everyone seems to have an opinion. Since God doesn't explain the meaning, apparently it's not important for us to know. Before this person comes to prominence believers will have been translated into God's presence. We will not have the slightest interest in the Beast or the False Prophet because we will be occupied with the Lord Jesus Christ in glory.

The reason God gave us any information at all, I believe, is so that believers alive in that day will have a clear identifying sign that the one in world power is Satan's masterpiece.

The diabolical nature of this dictatorial system will be worse than any in the history of the world. Why would God permit such a system to gain power? The answer, I believe, is found in the Old Testament prophecies of Zechariah.

Zechariah had been sent by God with a message of righteousness and an exhortation to the nation Israel, but Israel, after listening to Zechariah, turned away from him. So he asked them to evaluate his ministry and give him what they thought it was worth. They conferred and said, "What will we give this one to show our contempt for him and his ministry?" They recalled the law of Moses: if a man had a slave who had been gored by an ox, the master was to be paid thirty pieces of silver. They decided to show Zechariah what they thought of him. They began to count the coins into his hand—ten, twenty, twenty-eight, twenty-nine, and thirty. They valued him at the price of a dead slave.

Years later Christ came to the nation Israel to fulfill all that God had promised to Abraham and to David—the promise of a King, of a new heart, and redemption. But Israel rejected Christ and said to the Roman governor, "Away with him . . . we have no king but Caesar." They accused Him of treason. When Judas received payment for betraying Jesus, they began to count: ten, twenty, twenty-eight, twenty-nine, thirty pieces of silver. To Israel Christ was of no more value than a dead slave.

For rejecting His Son, God will bring them into judgment and deliver them into the hand of a false shepherd.

Though God will judge His people who rejected Jesus Christ as Messiah, He will also bring judgment on the Beast and the False Prophet. "The beast was taken, and with him the false prophet that wrought miracles before him, with which he deceived them that had received the mark of the beast, and them that worshipped his image. These both were cast alive into a lake of fire burning with brimstone. And the remnant were slain with the sword of him that sat upon the horse" (Rev. 19:20). Eternal separation from God will be meted upon the Beast, the False Prophet, and all who follow in their footsteps.

10

The Rise and Demise
of Russia

Ezekiel 38:1–39:29

TO SUGGEST THAT the Bible has anything to say about Russia and Communism would seem sheer fanaticism. Yet God made some very clear revelations in His Word about the rise of the great power to the north of Palestine that will shake the peace of the world. A considerable portion of Scripture is devoted to revealing the program of the end times.

One of the great powers of the last days will belong to the "king of the North." World power will be divided into four great sectors just before the Lord's return. These powers have names related to the land of Palestine, the hub of all prophetic Scriptures. There is, first of all, a power known as the "king of the North," because his domain lies to the north of Palestine. Another power, known as the "king of the South," lies to the south of Palestine. The head of the Federated States of Europe comes from the west. And the "king of the East" is a coalition of powers to the east of Palestine—Oriental or Asiatic powers from beyond the Euphrates River.

Two chapters that immediately come to mind are Ezekiel 38 and 39, Ezekiel's prophecy concerning the restoration of Israel to the land of Palestine.

Ezekiel prophesied during the time the children of Israel were in Babylonian captivity. They had forsaken Jehovah, the true God of Israel, and were under God's judgment because of their idolatry. God sent Ezekiel to this downtrodden and downcast people to remind them that God had a purpose for them. He had promised Abraham He would give the Jews the land of Palestine; and He had promised David He would give Israel a king forever. Through Ezekiel, God promised Israel that the desolated land of Judah and the destroyed city of Jerusalem would be occupied again and the city would be rebuilt as a testimony to the heathen around them (Ezek. 36:7, 10).

Later in the chapter, God said, "I poured out my fury upon them for the blood that they had shed upon the land, and for their idols wherewith they had polluted it: And I scattered them among the heathen, and they were dispersed through the countries" (v. 18). Instead of offering blood sacrifice to the true God, the children of Israel were offering human sacrifice to heathen deities. There was nothing left for God to do but punish the nation. Yet He said, "I will take you from among the heathen, and gather you out of all countries, and will bring you into your own land. Then will I sprinkle clean water upon you, and ye shall be clean: from all your filthiness, and from your idols, will I cleanse you. A new heart also will I give you, and a new spirit will I put within you: and I will take away the stony heart out of your flesh, and will give you an heart of flesh. And I will put my spirit within you, and cause you to walk in my statutes, and ye shall keep my judgments, and do them" (vv. 24–27).

That was the comforting hope given to this dispersed and chastened nation of Israel. They were punished because of their sins. God scattered them among the heathen, and the heathen nations ground them under their heel, oppressed them, and destroyed their land. But God promised to bring spiritual cleansing and to turn their hearts to Himself. He would wash away their sins and iniquities and remember their transgressions no more. They will be His people and He will be their God.

Ezekiel revealed how God will restore Israel to their land under their own king. The key to this great sweep of prophecy is contained in chapters 37 through 39.

To reveal something of His program, God set Ezekiel where he could look over a great valley full of dry, parched bones. It was not designed to appeal to the prophet's aesthetic sense. Death had done its work on the bones; there was no life left. A question came to Ezekiel from God, "Can these bones live?" The natural response would have been, "Of course not. Life is gone. Those bleached bones are the evidence of a former life that no longer exists." But the prophet said, "God, *thou* knowest." That was the same as saying, "God, if these bones ever live, it isn't going to be the work of a prophet; it will be the work of God. You alone know what's going to happen to these bones."

God told the prophet to do a very strange thing: preach to the bones. That was the strangest sermon and the strangest congregation in the history of preaching. Preachers have preached to deaf congregations before, but none has ever preached to an audience whose deafness was quite so obvious, nor to a congregation where there was less prospect of getting results. But God said, "Prophesy to these bones, and say unto them, 'O ye dry bones, hear the words of the Lord'" (v. 4). How could dry bones hear any words from the Lord? Humanly speaking, it was impossible. But our God is a God of miracles. He can give a dry bone an ear to hear, and He can give one who is spiritually dead the ability to hear a transforming message. So Ezekiel preached to the bones. "Behold, I will cause breath to enter into you, and ye shall live: and I will lay sinews upon you, and will bring up flesh upon you, and cover you with skin, and put breath in you, and ye shall live; and ye shall know that I am the Lord" (vv. 5–6). Ezekiel proclaimed that God was going to make those dry, lifeless bones live again. He would reverse the process of death and corruption.

In perfect obedience to the Word of God, Ezekiel said, "So I prophesied as I was commanded." As a result, there was a noise and a shaking, and the bones began to come together, "bone [came] to his bone. And when I beheld, lo, the sinews and the flesh came up on them, and the skin covered them above: but there was no breath in them" (v. 8). The prophet preached an earthshaking sermon, but his congregation still showed no signs of life. The bones were brought together and enclosed in flesh, but they were still dead. There was no life in them.

The prophet was told to keep on preaching. "Prophesy unto the wind [*the spirit*, as it might be translated], prophesy, son of man, and say to the wind, 'Thus saith the Lord God: Come from the four winds, O breath, and breathe upon these slain, that they may live.' So I prophesied as

He commanded me, and the breath came into them, and they lived, and stood up upon their feet, an exceedingly great army" (v. 9). That which was physically dead became alive, and the prophet looked upon this vast army of those who had been dead but now were alive.

Some interpret this as a promise of the resurrection of the physical body, but I do not believe that is what this passage teaches. God explained to the prophet what it meant. He said, "The bones are the whole house of Israel" (v. 11). Israel had been out of their land. They had been buried among the Gentile nations. They were, in a sense, in the grave, devoid of spiritual and national life. But God promised to bring Israel to life again; those bones represented the whole house of Israel.

At the time of Ezekiel's prophecy, Israel was saying, "Our bones are dried up and our hope is lost. We are cut off from the land." God sent the prophet with a message to assure the people that the God who made a promise to Abraham and David was faithful and *would* fulfill His word to them. God said, "I will open your graves, and cause you to come up out of your graves, and bring you into the land of Israel. And ye shall know that I am the Lord, when I have opened your graves" (v. 12). Then the explanation is given to us again: "Say unto them, 'Thus saith the Lord God; Behold, I will take the children of Israel from among the heathen, whither they be gone, and will gather them on every side, and bring them into their own land'" (v. 21).

In chapter 36 God said Israel would be punished for an extended period of time because of idolatry. Israel wanted to know how God would bring them back to the land. The prophet told them what the Lord had to say.

First, there will be a miraculous regathering of the children of Israel back to the land. God will do a special work to bring a scattered, buried people out of their graves among the Gentiles and back to their own land. God will bring them to a knowledge of Himself and impart spiritual life to them.

From that point, we go to chapter 38 to study an event that God will use to bring people who are physically alive but spiritually dead to a knowledge of Himself.

Israel today is being put back into the land, as described in 37:8. I believe we have heard, as the prophet heard, the first rattling and shaking of those bones. The restoration isn't complete by any means, but the first bones have come back. There is, however, no breath in them. They are without spiritual life.

To turn the people back to Jehovah before Jesus Christ returns to reign, God will do a miraculous work to open the blind eyes of Jews and Gentiles and to convince them that God is truly sovereign. Beginning in chapter 38, the prophet outlined the object lesson God will use to bring the people back to Himself.

"The word of the Lord came unto me, saying, 'Son of man, set thy face against Gog, the land of Magog, the chief prince of Meshech and Tubal, and prophesy against him'" (vv. 1–2). God told the prophet to deliver a message against a man named "Gog" and his kingdom "Magog." The statement follows, "the chief prince of Meshech and Tubal," or, more literally, "Set thy face against Gog and the land of Magog and Rosh, with princes of Meshech and Tubal."

The word translated "chief" may be either a common noun or a proper noun. If it is a common noun, it ought to be translated "prince." If it is a proper name, it ought to be translated "Rosh." God said, "Thus saith the Lord God, Behold I am against thee, O Gog, and against Rosh, the prince of Meshech and Tubal" (v. 3).

Genesis 10 helps us identify these names. "Now these are the generations of the sons of Noah, Shem, Ham, and Japheth." Verse 2 lists the sons of Japheth: Gomer, Magog, Madai, Javan, Tubal, and Meshech. The names referred to in Ezekiel 38 are all sons of Japheth. This is significant, I believe, because ethnologists tell us that the Japhethites, after the flood, migrated from Asia Minor to the north, beyond the Caspian and Black Seas. Instead of going to the south, as did the Shemites and the Hamites, the Japhethites moved to the north and became the people of the north. They went beyond the Caucasus mountains and established their civilization beyond the Black Sea and the Caspian Sea, in the area of Rosh, which we know today as modern Russia. Gog and Magog and Rosh and Meshech and Tubal, I believe, comprise present-day Russia.

A great military movement under the leadership of Gog, the prince of Rosh, is described in Ezekiel 38:4: "And I will turn thee back, and put hooks into thy jaws, and I will bring thee forth, and all thine army, horses and horsemen, all of them clothed with all sorts of armour, even a great company with bucklers and shields, all of them handling swords." Verses 5 and 6 list the allies of Russia: Persia, Ethiopia, Libya, Gomer, Togarmah, and all his bands. We have no trouble identifying Persia; we know it today as Iran, a country situated east of Palestine. But Ethiopia and Libya are used in two distinctly different senses in the Old Testament. Nations in Africa known as

Ethiopia and Libya continue to the present time. But in Old Testament times there were states adjacent to Persia known as Ethiopia and Libya. When Moses fled from Egypt after slaying an Egyptian, he went into the wilderness and married an Ethiopian. He did not go south into the African Ethiopia; he went into the Ethiopia located in the Arabian Peninsula. When Ezekiel spoke of Persia, Ethiopia, and Libya, I believe he was speaking of Arab states.

Verse 6 tells us that there will be "many people with thee." From this we understand that Russia, when it is ready to move against Palestine, will have the Arab states as allies. This suggests that Western influence will decrease in the Arab states and the power and influence of Russia will increase until the Arab states are in the communistic camp. When the head of the Federated States of Europe backs the Jewish claims to Palestine and guarantees its rights in the land of Palestine, the Arab states will turn to Russia and go completely into that camp.

"Be thou prepared, and prepare for thyself, thou, and all thy company that are assembled unto thee, and be thou a guard unto them" (v. 7), or as it is better translated, "Be thou a commander unto them." Russia will become the head of a coalition of states that will include the Arab states of the Near East.

"After many days thou shalt be visited: in the latter years thou shalt come into the land that is brought back from the sword" (v. 8). The latter years refer to the tribulation. This movement of the northern army into the land of Palestine, therefore, takes place after the church meets the Lord in the air. The "latter years" in Old Testament prophecy refers to the period of time just before Christ's second coming. In those "latter years" Israel will come into the land, that is, the land of Palestine, because the head of the European states has, by that time, given Palestine back to the Jews.

Gog will say, "I will go up to the land of unwalled villages; I will go to them that are at rest, that dwell safely" (v. 11). Israel will be trusting the Federated States of Europe to guarantee their safety when Russia moves against Palestine to take possession of the great mineral wealth and natural resources that are there.

Those outside of Gog's camp will watch Gog invade Palestine to take all the wealth. Sheba and Dedan and the merchants of Tarshish (the Western power, or the Federated States of Europe) will be upset when Russia moves into Palestine and will say to Gog, "Art thou come to take a great spoil?" But their objection will mean nothing, for we read in verse 16, "And thou shalt come up against my people of Israel, as a cloud to cover the land; it shall be in the latter days, and I will bring thee against my land, that the heathen may know me, when I shall be sanctified in thee, O Gog, before their eyes."

When Russia begins to move against Palestine, the Western powers apparently will be too weak to prevent it. Russia will be in command. But God will be working according to His own will. He will bring Russia into Palestine to use Russia as the greatest object lesson this world has ever seen.

If there is any comfort or consolation in this present world scene, it is what is given to us in verse 16. Russian Communism is under God's authority and cannot go one step beyond His purposes. No matter how dark this world situation looks, it has not gotten out from under God's sovereign authority. God is letting all things progress according to His will. People think they are developing their own plans and purposes, but it is all according to *God's* plans, so that He may demonstrate that He is without equal.

When God causes Gog to march into Palestine, overriding the objections of the West, the army will cover the land as a cloud, bringing death, desolation, and bloodshed. They will plunder a land that has been resting safely and securely.

After Russia makes her conquest, God will begin to move (v. 21). Up to this time, it has been Gog on the move. But God will take His turn. "I will call for a sword against him [Gog], throughout all my mountains, saith the Lord God, and every man's sword shall be against his brother. And I will plead against him with pestilence and with blood; and I will rain upon him, and upon his bands, and upon the many people that are with him, an overflowing rain and great hailstones, fire, and brimstone. Thus I will magnify myself, and sanctify myself; I will be known in the eyes of many nations, and they shall know that I am the Lord" (38:21–23).

Sodom and Gomorrah were two of the world's most well-known cities. They became famous when God poured fire and brimstone on them and blotted them out because of their sin. To this day people look for the location of Sodom and Gomorrah, but God so completely destroyed it that the ruins have never been found. As God poured fire and brimstone on Sodom and Gomorrah, so He will devastate Russia, but on a vastly greater scale. The world will see evidence that God is sovereign over this earth.

"And I will send a fire upon Magog, and among them that dwell carelessly in the isles: and they shall know that I am the Lord" (39:1–6) suggests that this judgment will not fall on the invading army only, but also on the head-quarters of that power and on all those who supported it. Millions will be removed in a moment of time.

This will be God's divine judgment on godless, atheistic Communism. God will demonstrate that no one can repu-diate Him and live. Verse 9 describes the extent of this judgment. It will take the Israelites seven years to collect the debris and dispose of it. And death will be so extensive that it will take seven months to bury the dead (vv. 11–12).

This all happens, I believe, at the middle of the tribula-tion. Russia will want the land of Palestine, given to the Jews by the head of the Federated States of Europe, but will do nothing about it for probably three years. Then Russia and its allies will invade Palestine. At this time, in the middle of the tribulation, God will wipe out Russia and Russian Communism with all of her allies. The Federated States of Europe then will move into the vac-uum created by the overthrow of Russia and will rule the earth. There will be one world government, one world religion, one world dictator, with no competition from the "king of the North," or Russia.

From these passages, I conclude that Russian Commu-nism will increase but that it will not take over the West-ern sphere of influence. There will be a stalemate between these two great powers until Russia feels confident that it can win a great world war. They will make the first thrust in that military campaign by invading Palestine. But God will intervene and wipe them out.

I do not hesitate to declare that Russian Communism—though it will increase, become more powerful, and bring much of the world under its sphere of influence—is a doomed system that God will judge.

Two great groups will be aroused by the destruction of Russian Communism. First, Israel will see it and say that the one who brought that judgment is their God, the one who will send their Messiah. Many in Israel will turn to God and become His servants and witnesses during the last years of the tribulation, bringing multitudes to a saving knowledge of Jesus Christ. Second, the nations of the earth will see this sign and many will acknowledge that Jesus Christ is Lord and Savior (Ezek. 29:27–28).

God permitted Russia to come to power so that He could destroy it and demonstrate that He is God, so that multitudes would come to know Him, the only true God, through Jesus Christ whom He has sent.

11

The Campaign of Armageddon

Daniel 11:40–45

"WE ARE ON the very brink of Armageddon," a commentator once said. Every time we hear swords rattle we wonder if they herald the coming of the great battle, the unprecedented holocaust called Armageddon.

Why

When God chose Israel as His repository of divine truth and His instrument for making Himself known to the nations of the earth, the nation became the target of satanic attack. The history of Israel is the history of Satan's attempts to wipe out God's chosen people and thereby destroy God's program of redemption.

In the time of Christ, Israel was ruled by the cruel oppressor, the Roman Empire. Israel's national rights of self-government and self-determination had been abrogated; they were subjected to the iron fist of Rome. Yet Jesus Christ came to reaffirm and reiterate the promises of

God to the nation Israel: that God would raise up a King who would deliver them from sin and bring them into the Millennial Kingdom.

But Israel rejected its Messiah. When confronted with a choice between Christ and the Roman emperor, the people said, "Away with this man, we have no king but Caesar." The sentence for their rejection was the desolation of Jerusalem and the Jewish nation.

The prophetic Scriptures reveal that the plight of Israel will become increasingly serious. The people must suffer a great deal more before the Son of God will redeem them and bring them into their land, where God will reign over them. During the tribulation, Satan will let loose upon this earth unprecedented persecution. Revelation 12 tells about the satanic movement that will try to obliterate every Jew. In the middle of the seven-year tribulation, or three and one-half years before Christ returns, there will be a movement of unrivaled wrath against Jews.

John wrote more about this movement in Revelation 16:13: "I saw three unclean spirits like frogs come out of the mouth of the dragon." Frogs dwell in the deep, or mire, so this is a picture of something that comes out of the pit; it is the manifestation of the purpose and plan of Satan, who works through the Beast and the False Prophet. These three form a trinity from the pit. "They are the spirits of devils, working miracles, which go forth unto the kings of the earth and of the whole world, to gather them to the battle of that great day of God Almighty" (v. 14).

Satan is putting his plan into operation. He knows He must exterminate every Jew to thwart God's plan. If Christ comes, as He promised, to reign over the seed of

Abraham and David, there will be no place for Satan and his kingdom.

How

To accomplish this, Satan will move nations against Palestine and bring organized military powers to exterminate them. The Beast and the False Prophet will issue a summons to the kings of the earth to gather them to battle in a place called Armageddon (v. 16). The word translated "battle of this day" (v. 14) is different from the normal Greek word translated "battle." A battle is one isolated meeting of two armies. The Greek word used here means a campaign. John described the campaign that will consummate at Armageddon.

Where

The prophecies of Ezekiel tell us, "Thou shalt ascend and come like a storm, thou shalt be like a cloud to cover the land" (38:9). Before it is finished, this campaign will sweep over the whole land of Palestine. *Armageddon* is the Hebrew word that means the mountain of Mageddo, which lies north of Jerusalem in the northern part of Palestine. The valley of Mageddo is a great extended plain that stretches from the Mediterranean Sea eastward across the northern part of Palestine. Napoleon called this plain the world's greatest natural battlefield. He said it had sufficient room for the armies of the world to maneuver.

The prophet Joel revealed more about the site of this battle. "I will also gather all nations, and bring them down to the valley of Jehoshaphat" (3:2). The Valley of Jehoshaphat was the portion of Palestine that went from Jerusalem to the east of Jordan and then northward. It was the trade route from Jerusalem to Assyria in the north and is the second part of Palestine that will be crossed and re-crossed by marching armies. The campaign will reach from Armageddon on the north to the valley of Jehoshaphat on the east.

Isaiah also had something to say about this great campaign: "Come near, ye nations, to hear; and hearken, ye people: let the earth hear, and all that is therein; the world, and all things that come forth of it. For the indignation of the Lord is upon all the nations, and his fury upon all their armies: he hath utterly destroyed them, he hath delivered them to the slaughter. Their slain also shall be cast out, and their stink shall come up out of their carcasses and the mountains shall be melted with their blood" (34:1–3). "The sword of the Lord is filled with blood, it is made fat with fatness, and with the blood of lambs and goats, with the fat of the kidneys of rams: for the Lord hath a sacrifice in Bozrah, and a great slaughter in the land of Idumea" (v. 6). "Who is this that cometh from Edom? with dyed garments from Bozrah? . . . Wherefore art thou red in thine apparel, and thy garments like him that treadeth in the winefat?" (63:1).

Putting these passages together, we learn that the land of Edom also will be included in this campaign of Armageddon. Edom is the state that lies south and east of Jerusalem, below the Dead Sea.

Of this great campaign the prophet Zechariah said, "Behold, I will make Jerusalem a cup of trembling unto all the people round about, when they shall be in the siege both against Judah and against Jerusalem" (12:2). "I will gather all nations against Jerusalem to battle" (14:2).

When we put all this together, we realize that the campaign of Armageddon will cover the whole land, even as Ezekiel 38:9 says. It will begin on the plain of Mageddo to the north, go down through the valley of Jehoshaphat, include the land of Edom to the south and the east, and have its center in Judea and Jerusalem in the central part of Palestine.

John painted a gruesome picture of this immense battlefield: "And blood came out of the winepress, even unto the horses' bridles, by the space of a thousand and six hundred furlongs" (Rev. 14:19). Sixteen hundred furlongs is approximately two hundred miles, and from the northern to the southern part of Palestine is approximately two hundred miles. According to John's prophecy, the land of Palestine will be given a bloodbath of unprecedented proportions. Blood will flow from Armageddon at the north, go down through the valley of Jehoshaphat, cover the land of Edom, and wash over all Judea and the city of Jerusalem. John described this scene of carnage as blood flowing to the depths of the horses' bridles. It is beyond human imagination to see a lake of blood that size, all drained from the veins of those who followed Satan to try to exterminate God's people and keep Christ from His rightful throne.

Who

The Battle of Armageddon will be fought by four world powers.

After the church is translated into the presence of the Lord, the nations of Europe will unite to protect themselves against the "king of the North," Russia. This European confederacy is the first great power. The leader of the Federated States of Europe will give the land of Palestine to the Jews for their homeland and pledge to protect the integrity of Israel, as discussed in earlier chapters. This means that an alliance is formed between Palestine and the "king of the West," or the head of the Federated States of Europe.

The second great political power, which we also studied previously, is called the "king of the North" (Ezek. 38–39), or the Russian confederacy. This confederacy will eventually join with the Arab states of the Middle East.

The third great world power, the "king of the South" (Dan. 11), is Egypt, with whom the Arab nations will be allied.

A fourth great coalition of nations, referred to as the "kings of the East" (Rev. 16:12), are nations from beyond the Euphrates.

When

Daniel 11 outlines the events leading to the Armageddon campaign. Verses 36–37 tell about the ruler of the Federated States of Europe. The only God he recognizes is the god of war; the only power to which he bows is the power of the European confederation, which he heads. He has given Palestine to the Jews and guaranteed to protect their rights to it.

The Jews have been in their land for several years, congratulating themselves that they have entered into rest and security. The reason the Jews are willing to worship a Gentile and accept him as their Messiah is that their eyes have been blinded to the truth. When someone gives them their land and brings an end to their warfare, they will feel they do not need anyone else. And so God will send the events of Armageddon to chasten them.

"At the time of the end the king of the south shall push at him" (v. 40). The phrase "the time of the end" refers to the end of God's program for the Jews, the end of the period just before Messiah comes to set up His kingdom. The "king of the South," Egypt, is the nation Israel was in bondage to for more than four hundred years. Daniel, writing more than five hundred years before the birth of Christ, told us that the final conflict in world history will begin when Egypt sets the spark to this tinderbox and starts the campaign of Armageddon.

Verse 40 also says that "the king of the north shall come against him like a whirlwind." This is Russia. So Egypt and Russia will meet at Jerusalem and completely destroy the city. Evidently Russia, who has been sitting up north, wants to start a world war. They suggest that Egypt and the Arab nations have a right to the land the Jews occupy. Although the Russians have no pretext for invading Palestine, Egypt does. Russia promises that if Egypt will march against the Jews from the south, they will sweep down from the north and join Egypt in the destruction of Jerusalem.

That is why Revelation 14 says the Jews have to flee out of Palestine and seek refuge among the nations of the earth because of the thing that Satan brings to pass. He will try to destroy Israel by bringing Russia and the Arab states against the Jews in Palestine.

From our study of Ezekiel 38 and 39 we learned that these armies, after destroying Jerusalem, will withdraw to the plain of Mageddo, or Armageddon, in northern Palestine. There God will pour out fire upon that Russian-

Egyptian alliance, upon the Communistic federation, and wipe them out as He wiped out the wicked cities of Sodom and Gomorrah, with fire and brimstone.

This will leave the Federated States of Europe as the great world power. The Russian Communistic bloc will be obliterated three and one-half years before the Lord Jesus returns. So the head of the Federated States of Europe will begin to move into the glorious land.

"He shall enter also into the glorious land, and many countries shall be overthrown" (Dan. 11:41). I believe the "he" in this verse refers back to verse 36. If it referred to the Russian-Egyptian alliance, I believe it would have said "they" instead. But it says "he," and so I take this to be "the willful king" who will enter the glorious land of Palestine. He has conquered the whole area occupied by the Arab states, but then "Tidings out of the east and out of the north shall trouble him" (v. 44).

This is where the kings of the East (Rev. 16) enter the campaign. "The sixth angel poured out his vial upon the great river Euphrates; and the water thereof was dried up, that the way of the kings of the east might be prepared" (v. 12). This alliance of nations is not identified in any way except that it comes from the east, beyond the Tigris and Euphrates rivers.

I believe this is a coalition of Asiatic nations who watched the Federated States of Europe dominate the earth after the destruction of Russia and do not want the federation to dominate them. According to Revelation 9:14–16, this army of Asiatic peoples, or Eastern confederacy, will be two hundred million strong. No wonder tidings out of the east and north trouble the head of the European confederacy. His supply bases are across the

Mediterranean Sea. And so, as Daniel tells us, "he shall go forth with great fury to destroy, and utterly to make away many. And he shall plant the tabernacle of his palace between the seas in the glorious holy mountain" (11:44–45). The glorious holy mountain is Jerusalem. The seas evidently are the Dead Sea and the Mediterranean Sea. Thus the head of the Federated States of Europe decides to meet this army by setting himself up in the mountains of Judea where there are natural defenses. Again Jerusalem is occupied and destroyed by another great invading army that sets its headquarters near Jerusalem. Zechariah described this in 12:2–3 and 14:1–3.

The consummation of this campaign is recorded in Revelation 19, where we find still another invasion of Palestine. This time it does not come from the north, south, east, nor west; it comes from outer space, from heaven itself. When the Federated States are ready to engage in combat with the invading Asiatic force, the sign of the coming of the Son of Man will appear in heaven (Matt. 24:30). The warring nations will immediately forget their animosity for each other because of their common animosity against God.

When the Lord Jesus Christ comes from heaven He will meet the two hundred million Asians plus unnumbered millions in the armies of the Federated States of Europe who are trying to prevent His return. Yet by the word of His mouth He will destroy all who shook their fists in the face of God and said, "We forbid You to send Your Son to reign over us." As if Satan, by amassing all humanity together, could prevent the culmination of God's plan.

As we read our newspapers and follow the developments in international crises, it is not stretching the imagination to say that the nations of the earth are aligned so that this series of campaigns could begin. It will not take realignment of nations nor changes in world politics. The stage is set for these events to unfold whenever God gives the signal and removes His restraint.

The world today is divided politically as follows: (1) the Western democracies; (2) the Communist bloc; (3) the Arab states; (4) the Oriental powers. All third-world nations are under the umbrella of one of these. Thus the stage is set for the program revealed for the campaign of Armageddon.

As far as the nations of the earth are concerned, we are living in precarious days. But as believers in Christ, we are living in the most glorious days ever. God has given these Scriptures to help those of us living in the last days to understand His purpose. Our hearts should not give way to fear. We can live in the expectation that before these events unfold, we will be translated into His glory, where we will worship the One who loved us and gave Himself so that we might have eternal life.

12

When the Nations Meet the Son of God

Revelation 19:11–21

THE LORD JESUS CHRIST introduced Himself as the Son of Man to whom God gave authority to execute judgment. "For as the Father hath life in himself; so hath he given to the Son to have life in himself; and hath given Him authority to execute judgment also, because he is the Son of Man" (John 5:26). No picture of Christ is more awesome than the one that shows Him as judge.

We have already discussed how Christ will meet the armies of the world at Armageddon, where God will destroy the northern confederacy with fire and brimstone, as He did Sodom and Gomorrah. He also will step into the world scene at the end of the tribulation and destroy the armies that are converging on Palestine. God the Father decreed (Ps. 2:2) that the Son will smite the nations of the earth and rule over the nations that rebelled against Him, for all might and authority and power have been given by God the Father into the hands of God the Son.

In the book of Revelation, we find several passages that speak of Christ as judge over the nations of earth. Revelation 11:15 pictures events at the close of the tribulation. The angels have been sounding their trumpets to announce the judgment of God upon this earth. As the last of the seven angels sounds his trumpet, "There were great voices in heaven, saying, 'The kingdoms of this world are become the kingdoms of our Lord and of His Christ; and He shall reign forever and ever'" (11:15). The kingdoms of this world referred to here are those that were brought under the power of the Beast in his one-world government. They are to be subjected to the authority of Christ.

Revelation 19 describes the coming of Christ to put down the last form of Gentile world power. "I saw heaven opened, and behold a white horse" (vv. 11–16). A rider on a white horse in prophetic Scriptures depicts one who goes forth to conquer, who subjugates another power to himself. This Rider will not come from one of the corners of the earth, for this is no earthly deliverer; this Rider comes from heaven to conquer the rebellious nations who have repudiated God's right to rule over them. The One who sits on this horse will be called "Faithful and True."

Jesus Christ is the *faithful* one because He is perfectly obedient to the will of God. He is the *true* one because He opposes the one who is the lie. The ruler of the Federated States of Europe has Satan, the father of lies, as his father. That satanic system is called THE lie in 2 Thessalonians 2. The faithful and true One will come to judge and make war. When Jesus Christ comes the second time, He will not come in humiliation, as He did the first time. And He will not be meek and lowly, unrecognized and unreceived. He will come as the One who has the right to **judge and** make war. God will send Him to wreak vengeance upon this godless earth and to bring desolation and destruction on those who have rejected God.

When He comes as conqueror His eyes will be "as a flame of fire" (Rev. 19:12). All through the Scriptures a flame of fire speaks of something that searches out, that judges. Fire can go into every crevice and cranny and we are helpless to set up a barrier against it. When the Lord Jesus Christ judges, it will be with a holy judgment that is irresistible. "On his head were many crowns" (v. 12). God has given Him authority to perform this work of judgment. He will deal with the satanic emissary who took the crowns of the nations for his own. Only Christ has the right to claim the crowns of government and the right to judge.

"He had a name written, that no man knew, but he himself" (v. 12). We would like to know the name but we don't. It is the name that God the Father gave God the Son when He commissioned Him to do the work of judgment. It may be related to John 5:28–29, which tells us that all judgment has been committed into the hands of the Son.

When He comes, He will be "clothed with a vesture dipped in blood" (v. 13) because He comes in judgment. He has already subjugated the armies of the king of the North. He has already put down the Edomites, the ancient enemies of Israel, as described in Isaiah 60. He will come to trample underfoot the last organized coalition of enemies arraigned against God. His name will be "THE WORD OF GOD." This name, given to Christ when He comes to judge, is the same as the name John used to introduce Jesus in his gospel: "In the beginning was the

WORD, and the Word was with God, and the Word was God" (John 1:1). A word is that which reveals the mind, heart, and will of an individual. At His first advent, when men were ignorant of God, Jesus Christ came to reveal the mind, heart, and will of God. He was called the "Word of God" because He revealed the truth concerning the person of God to people. When Jesus Christ comes to this earth to judge, He will come once again as the Word of God; He will reveal the holiness of God, and people will be judged for rejecting the revelation of God made through the Word of God.

When Jesus Christ comes to reign and judge, He will be accompanied by "the armies which were in heaven [that] followed Him upon white horses, clothed in fine linen, white and clean" (v. 14). These armies are explained in Hebrews, where we find a description of the occupants of the heavenly city, New Jerusalem. This city is inhabited by "an innumerable company of angels" (12:22); the "church of the firstborn" (12:23), that is, saints of the present age; the "spirits of just men made perfect" (12:23), that is, all the Old Testament saints; and by "Jesus, the mediator of the new covenant" (12:24). The armies from heaven are the inhabitants of the heavenly city that will come to witness the triumph of Jesus Christ when He manifests His authority and subjugates all things to Himself.

Verse 15 describes the judgment: "out of his mouth goeth a sharp sword, that with it he should smite the nations: and he shall rule them with a rod of iron." The phrase "he shall rule them with a rod of iron" is the same one used by the Father to the Son in Psalm 2:6. Jesus Christ, by a spoken word, will destroy the might of the coalition of nations gathered against Him who have shaken

their fist in God's face and said, "We forbid you to send
Jesus Christ into this world to reign." Christ will speak just
a word and all their military might will be wiped out.

At that time God will summon all the birds of prey and
say, "Come, and gather yourselves together unto the supper of the great God; that ye may eat the flesh of kings,
and the flesh of captains, and the flesh of mighty men,
and the flesh of horses, and of them that sit on them, and
the flesh of all men, both free and bond, both small and
great" (Rev. 19:17–18). God will bring judgment upon all
who have rejected Christ's authority. The nations of the
earth will be eliminated at the appearance of Jesus Christ
at the Second Advent.

The crushing of military might by God's Son so that He
might rule the kingdoms of earth is only one part of His
dealing with Gentile world power. Matthew 25:31–46 tells
us what will happen to the rest of the Gentiles living when
Christ returns.

Only those who have been born again, who have received Christ as Savior, will be accepted into His earthly,
millennial kingdom. Also, the tribulation will be a time of
unparalleled preaching of the Gospel. At the translation of
the church, or rapture, Christ will call to Himself every
living believer and will resurrect all who accepted Christ as
Savior between the day of Pentecost and the rapture. At
the moment of the rapture, not a single believer will be
left on earth. Yet there will be unprecedented preaching
of the Gospel during the seven years of the tribulation.
This shows the marvel of God's sovereign grace. Revelation 7 tells us that during the tribulation God will seal
144,000 souls, 12,000 out of each of the twelve tribes of
Israel.

When God wanted an apostle to take the knowledge of the Gospel of grace to the Gentiles, He reached down to Saul of Tarsus, who was on his way from Jerusalem to Damascus to kill every believer he could find. By His sovereign grace, God took a man who was blind to spiritual truth and gave him sight, who was in darkness and gave him light, who was in enmity against the Way, and made him Paul, the apostle. By transforming Saul of Tarsus into Paul the apostle, God prepared a vessel to carry His message to the Gentiles. God will do the same thing with 144,000 Jews, and He will send them to the ends of the earth.

But how will 144,000 Jews carry the Gospel of salvation to every nation in just seven years? It doesn't seem possible. When we send out missionaries they spend the first five years learning a language. But when God redeems the 144,000, He will have people who already know the language and customs of the people of the world. When they have their eyes opened to the knowledge of God, they will be ready to begin preaching. God will send these converted Jews into the world with the message that salvation comes only through the shed blood of Jesus Christ. As a result of their preaching, there will be those "which no man could number, of all nations, and kindreds, and people, and tongues, [who] stood before the throne, and before the Lamb, clothed with white robes, and palms in their hands" (Rev. 7:9–10).

The ones in white robes are those who "came out of great tribulation, and have washed their robes, and made them white, *in the blood of the Lamb*" (vv. 13–14). People will be saved during the tribulation period only through the shed blood of Jesus Christ. God will energize the chosen ones, and multitudes will be brought to the Lord.

The kingdom has been prepared for the multitudes of Jews and Gentiles who will accept Jesus Christ as Savior. But of those alive on the earth—those who have escaped the invading armies, survived the plagues and pestilences, avoided the wrath of the Beast, the judgment upon the armies at the Second Advent, and the visitations of wrath—there will be many who are not saved. The Son of Man must determine whom to take into His kingdom and whom to reject.

"When the Son of Man shall come in his glory, and all the holy angels with him, then shall he sit upon the throne of his glory" (Matt. 25:31). The throne of His glory is the throne God promised to David in 2 Samuel 7:6, the throne on which one of David's sons would sit to reign over David's nation.

"And before him shall be gathered all nations" (Matt. 25:32). I believe there has been much misunderstanding because of the English translation of "all nations." We have interpreted this as national groups such as Russians, Germans, French, Italians, North Americans, and South Americans. But the word translated here as "all nations" is normally translated in the New Testament as "Gentiles," which I believe is better: "Before him shall be gathered all *Gentiles*." This refers to a judgment upon all Gentiles who have not been killed during the tribulation. The King will separate the Gentiles into two groups—those on His right, the privileged place, who are referred to as sheep; and those on His left, the place of disfavor, who are spoken of as goats. There are only two divisions of Gentiles— sheep and goats.

Christ will say to the sheep, "Come, ye blessed of my Father, inherit the kingdom prepared for you from the foundation of the world: For I was an hungered, and ye gave me meat: I was thirsty, and ye gave me drink: I was a stranger, and ye took me in: naked, and ye clothed me: I was sick, and ye visited me: I was in prison, and ye came unto me" (Matt. 25:34–36). This invitation causes consternation and amazement. Those called sheep will think there has been a mistake. They will ask, "When saw we thee an hungered, and fed thee? Or thirsty, and gave thee drink? When saw we thee a stranger, and took thee in? Or naked, and clothed thee? Or when saw we thee sick, or in prison, and came unto thee?" (vv. 37–39). "Verily I say unto you," Jesus explains, "Inasmuch as ye have done it unto one of the least of these *my brethren*, ye have done it unto me" (v. 40).

The words "my brethren" introduce a third group. "My brethren," I believe, will be easily understood when we realize that Jesus Christ, according to the flesh, was a son of Abraham, a Jew. "He came unto his own [the nation Israel] and his own received him not" (John 1:12). From among the nation of Israel, 144,000 will be singled out at the beginning of the tribulation to represent Christ and proclaim His salvation. "My brethren" are the ones from Israel who have represented Christ by their preaching during the tribulation.

Revelation 13 adds to our understanding. There we learn that the Beast, when he comes to power, will pass an edict that no one can worship any God but himself. The False Prophet, allied with the Beast, will say that no one can buy or sell unless he submits to the authority of the Beast and accepts his mark. Christ's chosen preachers of

the Gospel will not bow to the head of the Federated
States of Europe. Thus they will be unable to buy or sell.
When they go into a village and announce salvation
through the shed blood of Christ and warn of His return
to earth as judge, some individuals will examine Scripture
to see if the things they proclaim are true. Some will be
convinced and will accept Jesus Christ as Savior. Then
they will share their food with the messengers, give them
clothing, and open their homes and give them lodging.
When these preachers are arrested for refusing to submit
to the Beast, the new believers will visit them in prison
and carry food to them.

When they minister to those who have told them the
Gospel, they display that they are truly children of God.
Christ accepts them into His kingdom on the basis of the
fact that they accepted the message of the Gospel and
proved their faith by the work they did for those who
brought the Gospel to them. These people were not saved
by works, for no one in history has ever been saved by
good work. But we can, by our works, *demonstrate* that we
have accepted the Gospel and trusted Jesus Christ as Savior. Although they did not realize that in ministering to
the messengers they were actually ministering to Christ,
He received it as acceptable service because they did it in
His name. Therefore He will say, "Come, ye blessed of my
Father, inherit the kingdom prepared for you" (Matt.
25:34).

Then He will turn to those on His left. With all of His
regal authority and His God-given power, He will say to
them, "Depart from me, ye cursed, into everlasting fire,
prepared for the devil and his angels" (v. 41). When they
plead ignorance Christ tells why they are being rejected:

"I was a stranger, and ye took me not in; naked and ye clothed me not; sick, and in prison, and ye visited me not" (vv. 42–43). They had a chance to minister to Him through the ones He sent, but they rejected the ministers of the Gospel as well as the Gospel they proclaimed. And so He will pronounce judgment on them. The results of this judgment are clearly stated: "These shall go away into everlasting punishment: But the righteous [the sheep] into life eternal" (v. 46).

When Jesus Christ sits on the throne of His glory, no one will question His right to judge. In bringing judgment on the assembled armies of the world, He will demonstrate that no one can resist His might and power. No individual alive at the Second Advent will avoid the judgment of the Son of God. Christ will receive into His earthly millennial kingdom those who accepted Him as Savior prior to His return, through the ministry of the 144,000. He will reject from His kingdom those who rejected salvation through His blood.

Everyone will meet Jesus Christ at one of two places: at the cross as Savior or at His throne as Judge. Those who accept Him as Savior have His promise that there is no condemnation or judgment to those who are in Christ Jesus.

13

The Judgment Seat of Christ

1 Corinthians 3:9–15

FEW DOCTRINES ARE of greater importance to the child of God than the doctrine of the judgment seat of Christ. If we were to examine the life of the apostle Paul, we would find that the controlling factor in his daily experience was his expectation of meeting the Lord Jesus at this judgment seat. Every step he took, every act he performed, every ministry he carried on, he did in anticipation of a day of reckoning.

In 2 Corinthians 5:9–10 the apostle Paul addressed believers. This is not a warning to those who have not accepted Christ as Savior and will one day stand before Him at the great white throne judgment. Paul is speaking of "we," which, according to verse 1, means those who have "a building of God, an house not made with hands, eternal in the heavens." This cannot refer to the unsaved because they have no habitation in heaven. "We" means those for whom "mortality might be swallowed up of life"

(v. 4). In other words, this body, being made subject to death and decay because of Adam's sin, will be resurrected and glorified. "We" are those who have received "the earnest of the Spirit" (v. 5), the foretaste, or the down payment of the Spirit. The Holy Spirit indwells believers only. And then "we" speaks of those who some day will be "absent from the body," but "present with the Lord" (v. 8). This too refers only to believers.

So we see from the context that the apostle was speaking of an event that relates to those who are children of God by faith in Jesus Christ.

Paul emphasized that this will be a universal examination for all believers when he said, "We must all appear." The word *all* means exactly what it says. No one who has accepted Jesus Christ as Savior will be exempted from this examination. It is *for* believers and it is for *all* believers.

What raises a problem for many is the word *judgment*. Whenever we use that word, we bring to mind a court scene where a judge sentences the guilty. No honest child of God claims to be without sin. No human is righteous. Even those who have accepted Jesus Christ as Savior fall frequently into sin. So when we think of the judgment seat of Christ we frequently picture ourselves standing before Christ as He metes out judgment. But I do not believe that is the teaching of this passage.

Several erroneous ideas have grown up out of the misinterpretation of the phrase "the judgment seat of Christ." Some picture this as a judgment to which every believer is subjected at death; it determines whether or not the person is permitted to enter heaven.

We realize immediately that this interpretation has no place in this passage because the apostle was speaking of those who have already received their eternal habitation, that is, the new glorified body (v. 1). They have already experienced death "swallowed up by life" and have received the earnest of the Spirit. They are already absent from the body and present with the Lord. This scene does not take place outside the gate of heaven. It occurs after the *believer* has been resurrected, translated, and glorified in the likeness of God's Son. The only judgment to which a believer will ever be subjected occurred on the cross. Christ bore our judgment, so we need not pass an entrance exam to get into glory. The presence of the Holy Spirit within us is our guarantee that we will be allowed in, and the righteousness of Christ given to us at conversion allows us to get in without judgment or examination. So we have to eliminate that popular but erroneous idea.

A second view, which is more prevalent but equally erroneous, says that the judgment seat of Christ is a time for God to punish believers for the sins they committed after they accepted Christ as Savior. This group believes that only sins committed prior to conversion are forgiven at conversion. According to this view, believers will be held responsible for every sin they commit after accepting Christ as Savior. At the judgment seat of Christ, therefore, God will examine believers' lives between conversion and death and mete out the appropriate punishment.

This too is a wrong interpretation of the teaching of Scripture in that it devalues the death of Christ. When God removes sin He does it completely, not partially. God said, "I have blotted out as a thick cloud thy transgressions" (Isa. 44:22). The brightest light we know, the sun, can be obliterated from sight by a cloud. This is one of the pictures God used to show that He will blot out the sins of believers through the blood of Christ.

The psalmist said, "As far as the east is from the west, so far hath he removed our transgressions from us" (Ps. 103:12). And the prophet Micah said, "Thou wilt cast all their sins into the depth of the sea" (Mic. 7:19). The density in the depth of the sea is so great that light cannot penetrate; and where no light can penetrate, there can be no sight. God was saying, "I am putting their sins where they can never be discovered again." Isaiah also said, "Thou hast cast all my sins behind thy back" (Isa. 38:17). This means "I will put their sins between my *shoulder blades.*" People cannot see between their own shoulder blades, so God was saying, "I am putting their sins where I will never see them again." The most glorious word in all the Bible about our sins is found in both the Old and New Testaments: "Their sins and their iniquities will I remember no more" (Jer. 31:34; Heb. 8:12).

There are many things we wish we could forget but can't; we have no power over our memory. The things we would like to forget come into our minds uninvited, and we have to rest in God's promise that He has forgiven those sins. Unlike us, God, by an act of His will, can dismiss from His memory every sin that has been covered by the blood of Christ. And when Jesus Christ washed away our sins in His blood, He did the job so completely and perfectly that God in His holiness can find no reason to condemn us. We are clothed with the righteousness of Jesus Christ.

The third view is related to the previous one and likewise is erroneous. People who believe it claim that God forgives only the sins that believers *confess.* When Christians refuse, neglect, or forget to confess sin, God will judge them at the judgment seat of Christ, make them confess, and punish them for every unconfessed sin. Everything said about the previous view applies here as well because this presupposes that our sins have not been completely and perfectly dealt with by the blood of Christ. It presupposes that God is recording all our iniquities so He can present them when we stand in His presence. This contradicts the holiness of God and the finished work of the Lord Jesus Christ.

The one who said "We must all appear before the judgment seat of Christ" also wrote that "there is therefore now no condemnation [judgment] to them that are in Christ Jesus" (Rom. 8:1). How can the apostle say there is "no condemnation," no judgment, and turn around and say "we must all appear before the judgment seat of Christ"?

In the original language the apostle's statement said, "We must all appear before the *bema* of Christ." The word *bema* was familiar to the Corinthians. Just outside the city of Corinth was a large Olympic stadium where athletes from all over Greece assembled periodically to compete in the Greek Olympic games. Within the stadium, in a prominent position, a platform was erected. During the contests, honored citizens and heads of state would sit on the platform to view the Olympic contests. The judges were down on the field where they could watch closely to make sure contestants observed every rule. Victors would be led by the judges from the scene of victory to this platform, which was called the *bema*. One of the honored citizens would then place an oak-leaf cluster or a laurel wreath as a chaplet on the victors' foreheads, or as a garland on their shoulders. The victors could wear this award during the rest of the Olympic games as a sign that they had competed lawfully and been triumphant.

Paul then was picturing the believer as a contestant in a race. Victors will be brought before the *bema*, where the Lord Jesus Christ sits, to receive their reward from Him. Thus the apostle was speaking not about judgment for sin, but reward for service. Paul said that believers must appear before the *bema* so "that every one may receive the things done in the body, according to that he hath done, whether it be good or bad" (2 Cor. 5:10).

The words "good or bad" at the end of verse 10 have contributed to the idea that this is a judgment for sin. The words were used in two senses in the original text. "Good or bad" could refer to sin and righteousness or to something that was usable or unusable, acceptable or unacceptable, apart from any ethical or moral significance. The apostle was saying that all believers will be examined to determine if what they have done is acceptable or unacceptable, whether it is suited to a designated use or not.

Sometimes a do-it-yourself carpenter will use a tool to do a job it was not designed to do. A pair of pliers is perfectly good when used for its intended purpose, but it doesn't work well as a hammer. When used to pound nails, it won't do much more than bend them. God wants us to use our lives for the purpose for which He designed us, and He will reward us accordingly. The apostle was not speaking of things that were morally good as opposed to morally bad, but of things that were useful as opposed to useless.

To determine what is usable and what is useless to God, "we must all be manifested." When we use the word *appear* we generally use it in a geographical sense. But the apostle was not talking about a geographical appearance in heaven. The word means "to be revealed," and he was saying "We must all be turned inside out so that what we were on the inside can be publicly displayed and so that everyone may receive according to that he has done, whether it be acceptable or unacceptable, usable or useless."

In 1 Corinthians 3 Paul used the figure of a contractor and a subcontractor to illustrate the same truth. He said, "We are laborers together with God: ye are God's husbandry, ye are God's building" (v. 9). God is the Contractor; Paul, Apollos, and Cephas, who had ministered to the Corinthians, were the subcontractors. Paul continued, "According to the grace of God which is given unto me, as a wise masterbuilder, I have laid the foundation, and another buildeth thereon" (v. 10). Paul had been brought in as a subcontractor to lay the foundation for the assembly in Corinth. Other men, following Paul, put stones in the superstructure. In verse 11 Paul said that Jesus Christ is the only foundation. People may build upon this foundation with gold, silver, precious stones, wood, hay, or stubble.

The apostle mentioned six different building materials, but they fall into two categories: indestructible and destructible. Gold, silver, and costly stones are indestructible; wood, hay, and stubble are destructible. The apostle affirmed to the Corinthians that the foundation had been laid and, because it was Christ, it was perfect. It is up to each believer to choose which type of building materials—destructible or indestructible—to use for the superstructure.

What brought up this question was a letter the apostle received about the Corinthian church being split because the people were comparing preachers, a pastime that is still popular today. One group said, "We like Paul's theology and logic." Another group said, "But Peter is so practical and down-to-earth; we like him." Others said, "We prefer the polished oratory of Apollos." Still others said, "We follow Christ alone!" The apostle looked at that sorry, divided mess and said, "Somebody slipped the wrong kind of building material into this building," and he warned them about the kind of stones they were putting into the superstructure.

"If any man build upon this foundation gold, silver, precious stones, wood, hay, or stubble; *every man's work will be made manifest.*" The word translated *appear* in 2 Corinthians 5:10 appears here as "be made manifest," or "shall be revealed." "The day" that shall reveal is the day of the *bema* of Christ when every believer's work will be subjected to examination. There will be a holy fire, kindled by God's righteousness, that will consume all that is destructible.

If I were to place a block of gold and a block of wood side by side, anyone could tell by looking at them which was which. Why then does God use such drastic means to determine what is destructible and what is indestructible? The reason is that God won't judge by appearance. He won't look at a thing and say, "That *looks* pretty to me. I will accept it." God is concerned about more than external characteristics. He judges motives more than acts.

The apostle pointed out two results of this examination. "If any man's work shall be burned, he shall suffer loss" (v. 15). Loss of what? Salvation? No! The apostle did not say,

"If any *man* shall be burned," but "If any man's *work* shall be burned." The individual will be saved, yet so as by fire. A person may have many works to put before the Lord, but if God's holy fire consumes it all, leaving the person with nothing, he will stand there shamefaced because he has nothing else to offer the Lord. He will suffer loss, but he himself shall be saved, yet as by fire.

Years ago I had the privilege of teaching a Bible class at the YWCA in Atlantic City. During that time a ravaging fire swept a five-block area of the city. The next day, after the Bible class was over, I walked down the boardwalk to the area that had been burned. What struck me as I viewed it was the complete devastation. I could not find any wood or combustible material. Nothing remained but layers of warm ash. I returned a week later with my wife. After class we walked to the fire scene. To my amazement the place looked as if it had been swept. An offshore breeze had carried the ashes away. I walked around the five blocks looking for charred timbers or residue of furniture, but I could find none. That which was destructible had been reduced to ash and blown away.

We find the second result of this examination in verse 14: "If any man's work abide which he hath built thereupon, he shall receive a reward," a reward for his work. So there are two results: loss of reward and reward.

What believers need to know about this teaching is how to determine what is destructible and what is indestructible. What did Paul mean when he used the words *gold*, *silver*, *precious stones*, *wood*, *hay*, and *stubble*?

I have already mentioned that it has nothing to do with appearance. Nor is it anything we might do to make something indestructible. Paul was saying that our attitudes and motives for doing things make the difference between gold and wood. Gold, silver, and precious stones are things God Himself created and placed in the earth. We can do no more than reap the bounty of God's provision. Wood, hay, and stubble are the things we plant, cultivate, harvest, manufacture, and use according to our will. I suggest, therefore, that what we permit *God* to do in and through our lives is the gold, silver, and precious stones spoken about here. In contrast, what we do for our own power and glory—because it suits our will or promotes our purpose—is the wood, hay, and stubble.

One Sunday school teacher teaches out of a heart tender to the Spirit of God. She is faithful in preparation and teaches for the glory of the Lord, not for her own pleasure, not to satisfy the person who asked her to do it, not to gain a reputation for being a good teacher. Another teacher wants to be in a position of prominence. She likes to be influential and wants to be respected for having an interest in spiritual things. These two teachers have done the *same thing* with their lives. But at the *bema* of Christ, God will say to the first one, "That is acceptable to Me because it brought glory to Me." To the other He will say, "That is unacceptable to Me because it brought glory to you only."

Some ministers preach because they love to do it, or because they like the influence, admiration, or respect it brings them. To them God will say, "I disown all of it. It is of no use to Me," and it will be swept away as wood, hay, and stubble. It is not the preaching that will win a reward; it is the motive for doing it. We must all ask ourselves, "What is my reason for doing this? Why am I involved in this ministry?"

We must ask the same question about activities other than ministry as well. "What is my motive for wanting this job?" Is it to satisfy my ego or to bring glory to God? "What is my motive for staying home with my children?" Is it because I want people from church to think well of me or is it to glorify God?

I repeat, God is not impressed by what we do; He's concerned about why we do it. No matter what we do, if we do it with a desire to glorify God, we will have God's reward. What we do in the factory, the office, at home, or at church will be counted by God as gold, silver, and precious stones if we do it to glorify Him.

It is not *what*, but *why*!

In speaking of these rewards, Scripture uses the figure of crowns. That image was meaningful to the Greeks because they thought of the Olympic crown winners wore through the streets to proclaim their victory. When we receive a crown at the *bema* of Christ, we will not put it on our heads and walk up and down the main streets of glory to compare crowns. The apostle John said that the twenty-four elders placed their crowns at the feet of the Lord Jesus Christ. As the hymn writer put it, "Upon the crystal pavement, down at Jesus' pierced feet, joyful I'll cast my golden crown, and His dear name repeat."

Crowns will not be given for us to possess; they are to be placed before the Lord as an offering. My deepest desire is that when I stand before Him in judgment the fruits of my life will be acceptable and that I will have something to put before Him as a thank offering for all He has done for me.

The book of Daniel has a passage related to rewards. "And they that be wise shall shine as the brightness of the firmament; and they that turn many to righteousness as the stars forever and ever" (Dan. 12:3). God manifests His presence and reveals His glory by a shining light. When God called us in Christ, He called us to manifest His glory. Based on Daniel's word that throughout eternity there will be those that shine, I believe our reward in eternity will be our capacity to manifest and radiate the glory of God.

Crystal chandeliers sparkle in radiant beauty when lit up. If you were to examine the chandelier, you would find it to be made up of many small bulbs: some 25 watts, some 50 watts, some 100 watts, some 500 watts. Each has a different capacity but each shines to the limit of its capacity. That chandelier is beautiful because of the total capacity of all the bulbs. In eternity, some of us will shine to the glory of God with a brightness of 25 watts, some with 50 watts, some with 100 watts, and some with 500 watts. All will contribute according to the capacity given to us at the *bema* of Christ.

Won't we be unhappy if we are surrounded by 100-watt bulbs and have only a 25-watt capacity? Not at all. The light will be so bright no individual lights will be detected; we will appear as one light. The shining of all believers will be a full and brilliant manifestation of the glory of God. It will not depend on individual lights; it will depend on our collective brilliance.

"It is required in stewards, that a man be found faithful" (1 Cor. 4:2). We usually read that as though it says, "It is required of stewards that a man be found *fruitful*," so we tend to estimate our reward by the number of people we have won to Christ. But the apostle did not say, "It is required in stewards that a man be found *fruitful*." He said we are to be found *faithful*. Whether God puts us in a factory, an office, a school, a home, a church, or a prison, He asks only one thing: faithfulness.

We must all be made manifest at the *bema* of Christ. Whether we receive or lose our reward depends on one thing—our faithfulness to Him now.

14

The Marriage of the Lamb

Revelation 19:7–16

ALL THE WORLD LOVES A LOVER. News of a wedding creates excitement. And the excitement increases as the tempo of life speeds up until the big day comes. That which interests us on earth is also the center of attention in heaven. Long ago heaven heard the news about a marriage and is waiting for the wedding of the Bridegroom and His bride. This wedding could never be imagined on earth; it is the wedding of the Son of God to the One the Father chose to be His bride.

If we, in our humanity, can enter into the experience of a couple pressing toward their wedding day, how much more must the host of heaven anticipate the day the bride will be presented by the Father to His Son.

The Scriptures have a good deal to say concerning this marriage, which will be consummated in heaven. But if we try to interpret it in light of modern customs, we will miss most of the meaning. To be able to picture the relationship we will have with Christ we must leave our twentieth-century culture and go back to the time when Christ lived.

There were three separate stages, or parts, of an Oriental marriage. The first stage was *betrothal*. Marriage was by contract. It was not an agreement between a young man and a young woman who had fallen in love and pledged their lives to each other. The couple who were to be married usually had nothing to say about the arrangements. The marriage contract was drawn up between the fathers. The parents *might* enter into the contract when asked to do so by a son who saw a young woman, thought she was lovely, and expressed an interest in her as a wife. But the fathers always made the arrangements. More frequently, the contract was drawn up by the fathers while the future bride and groom were still small children. Some records cite instances when a contract was drawn up before the couple was born.

This contract, called the "betrothal," was a legal enactment, duly signed before judges, which bound the parties to each other and could be broken only by a bill of divorcement. According to the gospels of Matthew and Luke, Joseph and Mary were betrothed. They had not been officially joined in marriage, and their union had never been consummated, but they were called husband and wife because of the betrothal. When it became evident that Mary was expecting a child that could not possibly belong to Joseph, Joseph had one of two choices. First, he could accuse her before the judges and subject her to the penalty of the law, which said that a person who was betrothed and then found to be unfaithful could be stoned to death. Second, he could "put her away privily," that is, he could give her a divorce. They were betrothed to each other, not married in our sense of the word, yet that betrothal could be broken only by divorcement.

The word used to describe the legal relationship of a young man and woman is also used to describe our relationship to Jesus Christ. The apostle Paul put himself in the position of a spiritual father to the Corinthians. He said, "I am jealous over you with godly jealousy: for I have espoused you to one husband, that I may present you as a chaste virgin to Christ" (2 Cor. 11:2). The word *espoused* is translated elsewhere in the New Testament as "betrothed." To Paul, the Corinthian believers were daughters in the faith, and Jesus Christ was a Bridegroom, a husband-to-be. Like a father, Paul had been instrumental in enacting a legal betrothal contract between his spiritual daughters and the Lord Jesus Christ. An indissoluble relationship had been instituted, and the apostle did not want the church to be drawn aside by false teachings. He feared they would be found unfaithful to their betrothed. So Paul said he was jealous over them with godly jealousy. He had betrothed, or espoused, them and he wanted them to continue in faithfulness until they were presented to the Groom.

In the spiritual realm, the betrothal of the believer to Christ took place in eternity past. Before we were born physically, we were betrothed by the Father to the Son. "Blessed be the God and Father of our Lord Jesus Christ, who hath blessed us with all spiritual blessings in heavenly places in Christ: according as He hath chosen us in him before the foundation of the world, that we should be holy and without blame before him in love" (Eph. 1:3). In this passage Paul pictured God the Father as choosing those whom He will betroth to His Son. When we look at this teaching, we see that the individual who has accepted Christ as Savior is part of what we refer to as the bride of Christ.

God is bringing together into a living, vital union every believer in His Son. The church is not an organization; it is an organism. The true church of Jesus Christ is composed of every individual who receives the gift of eternal life that God offers through His Son. Those who are blood-bought and blood-washed are brought together into a relationship with one another that we call the church, which is the bride of Christ. As it is natural for a bride to anticipate her wedding day, it is natural for the church to anticipate the day her Groom will take her into His presence.

A second part of the Oriental wedding was called the *presentation*. When the couple reached marriageable age, the young man would say, "Father, you have made legal arrangements for my marriage. Now it is time to send for my bride that this contract might be fulfilled." The father then would send a retinue of servants to the house of the bride. They would carry with them the legal contracts, present them to the father of the bride, and demand that he fulfill the terms of the contract and send his daughter to meet her groom. The groom's friends would accompany the bride in a procession to the groom's home.

The ceremony that followed was the "presentation." The bride's father would take the bride's hand and put it into the hand of the groom's father to signify that he had fulfilled his contract—he had delivered his daughter to the father of the groom. Then the father of the groom would place the bride's hand into the hand of his son to signify that he had fulfilled his part of the contract—he had delivered the bride to his son. At that point the couple

was legally married. Immediately after the ceremony—
which came months or even years after the betrothal—
they began their life together as husband and wife.

Scripture does not distinguish between the betrothal
and the presentation; it speaks of both of them as the
marriage. We depend on the context to determine which
stage is being discussed.

"Husbands, love your wives, even as Christ also loved
the church, and gave himself for it; that he might sanctify
and cleanse it with the washing of water by the word, that
he might *present* it to himself a glorious church, not having
spot, or wrinkle, or any such thing; but that it should be
holy and without blemish" (Eph. 5:25–27). The word *present* also appears in the last verse of the Epistle of Jude:
"Now unto him that is able to keep you from falling and to
present you faultless . . ."

The word used in these two instances is the word used
in the marriage ceremony when the father presented the
bride to the groom. The apostle Paul already mentioned
that we are betrothed to the Lord Jesus Christ. He then
moved to the second stage of the Oriental marriage and
said we also will be *presented* to Christ. He was picturing
God the Father's fulfillment of the legal contract He
agreed to at betrothal. The Father is responding to the
plea of the Son, "Father, give Me the bride You have
contracted for." The Father will send for the bride and
bring her, by resurrection and translation, into His home,
where He will present the bride to the Bridegroom.

We often refer to this event as the rapture of the
church—when believers are removed from this earth,
when the graves of believers are opened, death is overcome,
and we leave this mortal sphere to go into the presence of

the Father. But when we speak of the presentation of the bride to the Bridegroom, we are speaking of the moment the saints enter the Father's house, where the Father presents them as His gift of love to the Son.

According to Paul in Ephesians 5:27, when the Father presents the bride to the Son she will not have a single blemish. This confirms the perfection of the work of Christ. If we look at ourselves, we know that not one of us would make an acceptable bride for the eternal and infinite Son of God. We all have moral blemishes and the marks of sin's decay. Yet the work of God is such that when the Father presents us to the Son, we will be perfect.

Try to imagine some of those ancient presentation ceremonies. According to Oriental custom the bride was always veiled until the presentation—and not with a bit of lace netting that gave her face a soft illusion. The veil completely enveloped her. In many instances, the bridegroom had never seen the bride. He saw her for the first time after his father gave him her hand and with it the privilege of lifting the veil and viewing her face. There must have been more than one groom who said, "Father, what have I done to deserve this?"

But not so with Christ. The bride the Father presents to Him will be perfect, and with her the Son will be perfectly satisfied.

A third step in the Oriental marriage, like the other two, was frequently referred to as "the marriage." It was what we would call the *marriage supper*, or *marriage banquet*, or *wedding reception*. The bride was moving out of her home, out of her society, out from among her friends. She would be introduced into a new society; move into a new circle; meet new friends.

At the wedding reception, or wedding supper, the bridegroom would gather together all his friends and introduce his bride to those with whom she would mingle in future years. The length of the marriage supper was determined by the financial and social status of the bridegroom. It might last one or two days or a week.

God's Word includes many references to the marriage supper. "Jesus answered and spake unto them again by parables, and said, 'The kingdom of heaven is like unto a certain king, which made a *marriage* for his son'" (Matt. 22:1). The word *marriage* refers to the marriage feast. The king had prepared a banquet so his son could introduce the bride to his friends. But those who were invited were too busy to come. This was how the Lord pictured Israel's response to the first coming of Christ. He spread a banquet for them, invited them to partake of His bounty, but they were too busy with their own affairs to attend.

We find a similar story in Matthew 25 in the parable of the wise and foolish virgins. "Then shall the kingdom of heaven be likened unto ten virgins, which took their lamps, and went forth to meet the bridegroom. And five of them were wise, and five of them were foolish" (vv. 1–2).

Of the ten virgins only five had enough oil to keep their lamps burning until the groom came. The other five had to go buy more oil, and while they were gone the groom came and opened the door for the wise virgins to enter. Those who were unprepared were excluded. This illustration of the marriage feast speaks of the future consummation of Christ's program in the Millennium.

"Let us be glad and rejoice, and give honour to him: for the marriage of the Lamb is come, and his wife hath made herself ready" (Rev. 19:7). According to this passage, the purpose of this marriage feast is not to congratulate the bride nor to tell her how beautiful she looks. In the Oriental wedding the bride had little place. The bridegroom was in the place of prominence. They gathered, therefore, to honor him, not her. And the reason they honor Him is because "the marriage of the Lamb is come and his wife hath made herself ready."

John was speaking of an event that will take place at the Second Advent. During the age in which we live, the Spirit has been calling out a bride; we have been betrothed to Him. In Revelation 19, the rapture has already taken place and the bride has already been presented to the Bridegroom. But one important part of the marriage picture is still missing—the wedding feast, when the bride is introduced.

After speaking about the presentation of the bride, John moved to the subject of the marriage supper and said that "his wife hath made herself ready. And to her was granted that she should be arrayed in fine linen, clean and white: for the clean linen is the righteousness of the saints" (19:7–8).

A modern custom illustrates the meaning of "His wife hath made herself ready." After the marriage ceremony today it is common for the bride to slip away for a few minutes and change into her "going away" suit. She doesn't appear in public after the ceremony with the long flowing veil and white lace gown in which she was married. She has prepared her trousseau, giving thought and attention to what she will wear, so that when they appear together in public for the first time she will bring honor to her husband.

In the previous chapter, we considered the judgment seat of Christ and learned that after we are translated into

His presence every believer must be examined before the *bema* of Christ. Here John used another figure to refer to the same event. He said the bride-to-be prepared a trousseau, placing in her hope chest everything she will need for her first public appearance with her Bridegroom. God will examine her trousseau and remove from it anything that would not bring glory to the Groom. After the hope chest has been examined, the Bridegroom will tell His bride to put on the garment prepared for the occasion.

Verse 8 calls this garment "the righteousness of the saints." He was not speaking of the righteousness of Christ, in which we will always be clothed; he was speaking of that which we will put on *after* the judgment seat of Christ, to bring honor and glory to the Bridegroom. "She was arrayed in fine linen, clean and white: for the fine linen [in which she will appear with the bridegroom] is the righteousness *of the saints*." Imagine how a bride would feel if she spent years planning and preparing her wedding garments and discovered on her wedding day that a mouse had gnawed everything to shreds.

That scenario will be similar to what will happen at the judgment seat of Christ. We will appear there, thinking we have prepared many beautiful things to present to the Lord. But because we did them with our own energy or for our own glory, they will be unacceptable to Him. Much that we thought would bring glory to our Bridegroom will be destroyed.

"Blessed are they which are called unto the marriage supper of the Lamb" (v. 9). "The armies [of saints] which were in heaven followed upon white horses, clothed in fine linen, white and clean" (v. 14). When we put these two verses together, we discover that the wedding supper will be served on earth following the Second Advent of Christ. The wedding supper is God's name, or picture, for the millennial age, the millennial reign of Christ.

A wealthy man in Bible times might have a banquet lasting a week. God's feast will last one thousand years. Christ will appear as a Judge to separate the saved from the unsaved. He will appear as a King to reign. But to the bride for that thousand years He will be the Bridegroom. The Son of God will bring His bride, the church, back to earth when He comes so that He might be honored, adored, and glorified through her. The perfect bride will demonstrate what His grace does for sinners. And for the thousand years of the Millennium the Son will do what any bridegroom does—adore His bride and be adored by her.

In a former pastorate I had the privilege of working with a godly elder who had been married more than thirty years. In all my contacts with him I never heard him refer to his wife by any name other than "my bride." It sounds odd to us to hear someone be called "bride" after thirty years of marriage. But for the thousand years of the millennial age the church will be the bride of Christ. And the bride will be occupied solely with the Bridegroom.

> *The bride eyes not her garment*
> *But her dear bridegroom's face;*
> *I will not gaze at glory,*
> *But on my King of grace.*
> *Not at the crown He giveth,*
> *But on His pierced hand,*
> *The Lamb is all the glory*
> *Of Immanuel's land.*

15

The Great White Throne Judgment

Revelation 20:11–15

THE GREAT WHITE THRONE JUDGMENT, where sinners will stand in the presence of a holy and just God to give an account for their sins, is one of the most awesome revelations given to us in the Word of God. Our concept of the righteousness and holiness of God has been so adulterated and diluted that we see only God's love and think of Him as too kind to judge anyone for sin. But the Bible reveals that there must come a time when God will deal with this.

Genesis 3 records the fall of man. At the time of the fall, God pronounced a curse upon the serpent. "The Lord God said unto the serpent, 'Because thou hast done this, thou art cursed above all cattle, and above every beast of the field; and upon thy belly shalt thou go, and dust shalt thou eat all the days of thy life'" (v. 14). God also cursed Adam. "And unto Adam he said, 'Because thou hast hearkened unto the voice of thy wife, and hast eaten of the tree, of which I commanded thee, saying, "Thou shalt not eat of it" ' " (v. 17). Then God cursed the ground. "Cursed is the ground for thy sake; in sorrow shalt thou eat of it all the days of thy life; thorns and thistles shall it bring forth to thee; and thou shalt eat the herb of the field" (vv. 17–18). So there were three curses: upon the serpent (Satan), upon Adam (sinners), and upon the ground.

One of those curses was removed when Christ became a curse for us. "Christ hath redeemed us from the curse of the law, being made a curse for us: for it is written, cursed is everyone that hangeth on a tree" (Gal. 3:13). He became the Burden-bearer, the Sin-bearer, and He removed the curse that was on sinners. That is why the apostle Paul could write, "There is therefore now no condemnation [judgment] to them which are in Christ Jesus." The curse upon those who have accepted Jesus Christ as Savior has been removed because sin's debt has been paid. The apostle John said, "We may have boldness in the day of judgment: because as he is, so are we in this world" (1 John 4:17). When we accept Christ as our Sin-bearer, the curse that was upon us is borne away, the debt is paid.

But two curses remain: the curse upon the earth and the curse upon Satan. Also, sinners who spurn God's salvation are still under Adam's curse. Revelation 20 deals with the curses that remain. "I saw a great white throne, and him that sat on it, from whose face the earth and the heavens fled away; and there was found no place for them" (v. 11). The apostle John was speaking of an event that will occur after the millennial age.

When the Lord Jesus Christ comes to this earth to reign, before the Millennium, He will sit upon "the throne of glory" (Matt. 25:31). The significant thing about the millennial throne is that it is a *throne of glory*. The significant thing about the throne mentioned in Revelation is that it is a great *white* throne. Throughout Scripture, white symbolizes holiness and purity, the sinless character or quality of the essence of God. So here John was reminding us that Jesus Christ will be manifested in sinlessness, righteousness, and holiness as the eternal God so that He may judge in righteousness and holiness all who shall stand before Him.

John also said that "the earth and the heaven fled away [from the One who sat on the throne]; and there was found no place for them" (v. 11). This throne is not set up on earth; earth is gone. Neither is it set up in what we would refer to as heaven, God's dwelling place; sinners are not allowed into the presence of a holy God, nor will God allow them to defile heaven by their presence there. This throne is in an intermediate place, between heaven and earth, and the former heaven and earth are not part of the scene.

In the apostle Peter's day scoffers laughed at the doctrine of the second coming of Christ, saying, "Where is the promise of his coming? For since the fathers fell asleep, all things continue as they were from the beginning of creation" (2 Pet. 3:4). Because Jesus Christ did not return in Peter's day, people ridiculed the doctrine of the Second Coming. Peter said they were ignorant of God's patience, for God is longsuffering with sinners. Then he explained what God will do. "But the day of the Lord will come as a thief in the night; in the which the heavens shall pass away with a great noise, and the elements shall melt with fervent heat, the earth also and the works that are therein shall be burned up" (v. 10). The heaven and earth we know will be consumed by heat that will melt the elements.

When the atomic bomb was first developed and people saw its devastating effects, many turned to this passage and concluded that the earth would be destroyed by an atomic bomb. They concluded that the end of the world must be near. That makes spectacular headlines, but it isn't what Peter was talking about. He was referring to the fulfillment of the curse upon the earth pronounced in Genesis 3. Earth, the scene of man's rebellion against God, will be judged by God and purged so that it may be recreated and become the scene of the eternal glory of God.

God will carry out His sentence on the earth when "the heavens shall pass away with a great noise and the elements melt with fervent heat, the earth also and the works that are therein shall be burned up. Seeing then that all these things shall be dissolved, what manner of persons ought ye to be in all holy conversation and godliness, looking for and hastening unto the coming of the day of God, wherein the heavens being on fire shall be dissolved, and the elements shall melt with fervent heat?" (2 Pet. 3:10–12).

The scene that Peter described in detail is the one John referred to in Revelation 20:11. I am not predicting this will happen, but it is possible that God, by speaking one word, will bring this earth to dissolution using atomic fission. Hebrews tells us that all things in this universe are upheld by the word of His power. If Christ upholds all things by the word of His power, by another word He could cease to uphold it and dissolve everything. He will be given authority from God to carry out God's sentence upon the earth, the scene of man's rebellion.

That is the kind of God sinners will face. He isn't a kind and gentle grandfather who smiles benignly at the shortcomings and disobedience of his grandchildren! He is a God of infinite power and holiness, who must execute the sentence He passed on earth and Satan.

Of the second movement that occurs when God brings His judgments to their close, the apostle John said, "I saw the dead, small and great, stand before God" (Rev. 20:12). "The sea gave up the dead which were in it; and death and hades delivered up the dead which were in them" (v. 13). This is the picture of the resurrection of the wicked dead. To understand the meaning of what John saw in his vision of the dead standing before God we must consider God's program of resurrection.

Jesus said that the Father gave Him "authority to execute judgment also, because he is the Son of Man. Marvel not at this: for the hour is coming, in which all that are in the graves shall hear his voice" (John 5:27–28). Christ was speaking of the *universality* of resurrection. Every person, saved and unsaved, will be physically resurrected. "And they shall come forth; they that have done good unto the resurrection of life; and they that have done evil unto the resurrection of damnation [condemnation]" (v. 29).

The Lord was not telling us the *time* of the resurrections; He was teaching us the *fact* of resurrection. And the fact is, there are two kinds of resurrection: a resurrection unto life and a resurrection unto damnation. Elsewhere in Scripture they are referred to as the first and second resurrection.

Paul wrote about God's program of resurrection in his first letter to the Corinthians. "Now is Christ risen from the dead, and become the firstfruits of them that slept.

For since by man came death, by man came also the resurrection of the dead" (1 Cor. 15:20–21). Death came through Adam; the resurrection comes through Christ. "For as in Adam all die, even so in Christ shall all be made alive. But every man in his own order" (v. 22). The apostle then said that Christ is the firstfruits. He is the first part of the resurrection unto life and "afterward they that are Christ's at his coming" (v. 23).

This is one part of the first resurrection unto life. Another part, which we have already studied, will happen at the rapture, when all of the saved ones of this age will be resurrected and caught up to be with the Lord.

In Revelation John wrote, "Blessed and holy are these that have part in the first resurrection: on such the second death hath no power, but they shall be priests of God and of Christ, and shall reign with him a thousand years" (20:6). John was referring to the multitudes of believers who will be martyred during the tribulation. They will be resurrected at the second coming of Christ, but they will be part of the first resurrection, the resurrection unto life.

When we look at this much of the picture we see that Christ was resurrected nearly 2000 years ago as part of the first resurrection. At the rapture believers of this age will be resurrected; they too will be part of the first *resurrection*. Years later, at the second coming of Christ, Old Testament saints and saints martyred during the tribulation will be resurrected, and they too will be part of the first resurrection. All of these groups will be resurrected unto life. And this total program is the "resurrection unto life."

The first resurrection, the resurrection unto life, will be completed at the Second Coming. When Jesus Christ once again sets His feet on the Mount of Olives to reign during the Millennium, not one body of one believer—from Adam until that time—will be left in the grave. When Jesus Christ comes to reign, the first resurrection will have been completed and every believer will have been resurrected.

The only ones left to be resurrected at the great white throne are the bodies of unbelievers. So when John said, "I saw the dead, small and great. . . . And the sea gave up the dead which were in it; and death and hades delivered up the dead which were in them" (Rev. 20:12–13), he was speaking of the unsaved from the time of Adam to the end of the Millennium. Thus John was referring to the fulfillment of the curse on the unsaved (or sinners).

No grave will still have within it the dust of its occupant. Every individual will have been resurrected. Those who were resurrected to life will have been with Christ for over one thousand years. The unredeemed must now meet the Judge face to face. So the graves are opened, and there is a resurrection of all the wicked, for "death cannot keep its prey."

When John referred to "death" he was speaking of the power that held people and when he referred to "hades," translated "hell" in the King James Version, he was speaking of the place where these dead ones dwell. The multitudes of the wicked of all ages will be gathered together to stand before the One who recently demonstrated the enormity of His power and the righteousness of His judgment by dissolving the heavens and the earth. Who can imagine the fear of those called to stand before that holy and righteous Son of God to give account for their sins?

"The books were opened: and another book was opened, which is the book of life: and the dead were judged out of those things which were written in the books, according to their works" (v. 12). God is a divine Bookkeeper, and He has been keeping an unchangeable record through the annals of time. But for some reason He has been keeping two sets of books. These books are explained in the context. Verse 12 says that the dead were judged out of those things which were written in the books (plural), and verse 13 says they were judged according to their work. Putting the two verses together, we conclude that God is keeping a record of the works of sinners. Our own record was contained in them until it was purged by the blood of Christ.

God, in infinite grace, gave Jesus Christ to be our Sin-bearer, and when we accepted Him as Savior, He wiped clean the record of our evil works. When God looks at our record now, all He sees is that the judgment against us has been paid. The righteousness of Jesus Christ has been accrued to our account. I'm glad God is a faithful Bookkeeper who never forgets to make an entry.

But John was not speaking of those whose records have been cleared. He was speaking of the unsaved who stand before God to have the books opened. And when they peer into the record written there they find every detail of their lives recorded—all the sin, unrighteousness, and unholiness of their lives.

But there is a second book, and it is called the Book of Life. It is the register of those who have accepted Jesus Christ as Savior, and it is separate from "the books." God, by a double entry, used it to register the names of all who are saved. The Book of Life is a safety check. When an individual stands before God and the books are opened, there is the undeniable record of his sins, unrighteousness, and unworthiness to be received into the presence of a holy God. The record stands. And then, as though to demonstrate that no error has been made, God will take the Book of Life and look for the person's name. God won't find the name, so the sentence against the sinner will stand; the sinner did not accept God's provision of grace, so he or she must pay the sentence and bear the curse. The result is given in verse 15: "Whosoever was not found written in the book of life was cast into the lake of fire."

The basis for this judgment comes from verse 12: they "were judged out of those things which were written in the books, according to their works." People will not be sent into the lake of fire because they were murderers or liars. They will be sent there because they are unrighteous. Why then are the books opened? Why consult the record of a person's life? Because the record will prove the person's unrighteousness and demonstrate that all have sinned and come short of the glory of God. How black or how white a person's record is according to human standards does not matter. According to God, the record is imperfect, and all whose records do not measure up to the standard of the righteousness and holiness of God will have their part in the lake of fire, which burns forever.

People will not be sent to eternal punishment because of what they did, but because of what they were. They were rebels who would not avail themselves of God's grace. They would not receive the righteousness provided by God through His Son. And they will be sent to the lake of fire because they are not found written in the Book of Life.

"Death and hades were cast into the lake of fire" (v. 14). This is the third aspect of judgment that Christ will pass because of the curse—the judgment upon Satan. The Son of God—who pronounced sentence upon the earth and dissolved it by the word of His mouth, who pronounced sentence upon sinners for rejecting Christ as their substitute—will pronounce and execute judgment upon Satan. Satan has been robbed of all his prey; he does not hold one single individual in his grip. Satan and his domain are cast into the lake of fire.

Through this triune judgment, the Son of God will manifest that all authority and power and dominion and majesty belong to God, who lives forever and ever.

The lake of fire is the descriptive term used through the New Testament for the place of eternal punishment. It is beyond all human comprehension—a place of suffering, remorse, and eternal separation from God. But Satan is not king in the lake of fire. The apostle Paul said in Philippians 2 that when God set His Son on His throne "things in heaven, and things in the earth, and things under the earth" would be subject to His authority. The place of eternal punishment will be regimented by the authority of the Son of God. And every individual, resurrected to be judged and separated from God forever in the lake of fire, will acknowledge that He is King of kings and Lord of lords.

In the eternal state there will be no further rebellion, for every resurrected being will be in absolute subjection to the authority of the Son of God. "At the name of Jesus every knee should bow . . . and every tongue confess that Jesus Christ is Lord, to the glory of God the Father." And the inhabitants of the lake of fire itself will recognize the Savior they refused to acknowledge, and before whom they refused to bow while on earth.

The unsaved had the sentence of the second death passed upon them. The first death was not physical death; it was the separation of the soul from God at the time Adam sinned. When Adam sinned, he died spiritually. That was the first death. You and I were born spiritually dead, under the first death. The second death is the eternal separation of the soul from God. This sentence is passed at the great white throne. While acknowledging that Jesus Christ is Lord to the glory of the Father, they will yet be separated from Him, never to see His face, to enjoy His blessing and His provision, to fellowship with Him, to be like Him.

The Scriptures teach that there will be degrees of punishment in the lake of fire. Those who were entrusted with much but proved unfaithful to their trust will be "beaten with many stripes." Those who were entrusted with little will be "beaten with few stripes." But all will be beaten.

After John in his vision saw the judgments upon earth, sinners, and Satan, he saw "a new heaven and a new earth: for the first heaven and the first earth were passed away; and there was no more sea" (21:1). From this awesome scene of judgment, John brings us to the glory of our eternal habitation. "The tabernacle of God is with men, and he will dwell with them, and they shall be his people, and God himself shall be with them, and be their God" (v. 2). John saw a new earth as the habitation of all the redeemed of all the ages, where they are brought into this intimate fellowship with God the Father, the Son, and the Holy Spirit.

How blessed we are that John closed the book of Revelation, not with this picture of the great white throne judgment, but with the glory and the blessing of the presence of Christ in the new heaven and earth!

16

The Signs of the Times

Matthew 24:32–42

PEOPLE FREQUENTLY ASK ME, "Do you believe the coming of the Lord could be near?" In this chapter I will gather some of the teaching from previous chapters to explain why I believe the coming of the Lord could be very, very near.

Many years ago, I went on a riverboat excursion for a youth outing and picnic. We were planning to have singing and devotions on the back of the deck on the way home, but nature intervened. We were not very far along when the sky darkened and it began to sprinkle, and the sprinkle turned into rain, and the rain turned into a downpour. Needless to say, it broke up the meeting.

But the pilot didn't seem to mind a bit. He just kept the boat going up the river. We began to wonder how he could see to pilot the boat. Some of us made our way toward the bridge and got close enough to the pilot's cabin to see him standing at the wheel. Someone asked the pilot how he knew where he was going.

"You see that light there?" he asked, pointing.

Yes, we could see it.

"You see that one up there?"

Yes, we could see that light too.

"See the third one over there, to the left?" Our eyes followed his finger, and we could see the light he pointed to.

He explained, "I'll keep going up this river until those three lights merge together as one. When they come together like that, then I know I'm opposite the harbor where I want to go. The harbor has an auxiliary lighting system on the shore to get us in."

I'll go until the lights merge as though they are one, and then I'll know that we are near our destination.

Many individual lights are given to us in the Bible to reveal God's prophetic program. These lights won't herald the translation of the church, however; that event—the next in prophecy—will be unannounced. God has given no indication as to when it may come. He has simply said it will be suddenly, unexpectedly, in the twinkling of an eye. The apostles hoped the Lord would translate them in their day. It has been the hope of successive generations of believers through the ages of church history that the Lord might come in their day. It is our hope that the Lord may come at any time.

Meanwhile, certain things in prophecy are pressing rapidly toward fulfillment. A number of these events seem to be coming into focus, indicating that the lights are beginning to line up and merge into one. The prophetic events of God's program unfolded for us are the events of the tribulation period. The Word of God is very specific concerning the events that will take place on the earth after the church has been raptured.

Although the translation of the church will be without warning, foreshadowings of events that will consummate after the church is gone are already appearing on the world scene. And because of these things, I believe the rapture could and must be very near.

The Lord used an illustration from nature (Matt. 24:32–33) to show Israel the relation between the signs and the Second Coming. The Lord reminded the people how they knew when summer was near. When trees, divested of all foliage by the winter winds and ice, begin to show tiny green buds or swelling shoots, the people knew spring was near, and if spring was coming, summer could not be far behind.

That was what the Lord had in mind when He said, "Learn the parable of the fig tree. When his branch is yet tender, and putteth forth leaves, ye know that summer is nigh." The Lord was saying to the nation Israel that the revealed prophetic program contained in the Old Testament prophets, and in the prophecies of the New Testament as well, gives a number of events that will occur before the return of Christ, and these events will herald the second coming of Christ.

When we see buds burst, we know that the process of summer, though summer is still not here, has been set in motion and will culminate in the full leaves. Once the little green buds burst, we know the process will continue, without interruption, until the full leaf appears.

I do not mean to suggest that these signs must be *fulfilled* before the rapture takes place. But the Lord does say that if we study the Scriptures and look at God's movement in the affairs of nations, we will have some indication as to when God is setting the stage that will consummate in the coming of the Son of God.

Some events in world affairs point to the near fulfillment of prophecy and, therefore, have tremendous significance. The first significant event is the return of the Jews to Palestine. In chapter 5 we traced God's whole program for the nation Israel. In the promise to Abraham, God gave Palestine to the Jews as their inheritance. God told Abraham, and later the nation Israel through Moses, that if the children of Abraham obeyed God, God would bless them in their land. If they disobeyed God, He would bring chastening, and the chastening would take the form of expulsion from the land of blessing. God took the Jews out of Palestine under the Assyrian and Babylonian captivity hundreds of years before Christ.

The Jews were granted a measure of freedom in their land under the Romans at the time of Christ, but because of their rejection of Christ they were again expelled from the land of Palestine. That land has been under the authority of Gentile people from the time of Nebuchadnezzar to the present day. In 1948 the United Nations recognized the right of the Jews to Palestine as their homeland. For the first time in more than two thousand years Israel is recognized as an independent nation.

This has tremendous significance. When the tribulation begins, Jews will be in the land of Palestine looking for some world ruler to settle the continuing Arab-Israeli dispute. The dispute has not been settled by the United Nations, nor will it be settled by any other than Jesus Christ Himself. During the tribulation Israel will be back in their land in unbelief, oppressed by Gentiles, particularly Arabs, and will be looking for a deliverer. They will welcome the covenant of the Beast (Dan. 9:27) to protect them. We already see one little green bud on the tree signaling the approach of our Lord: an independent Israel in the land of Palestine today.

A second significant event that takes us into a great line of prophecy, which we studied in Ezekiel 38 and 39 and other parallel passages, is the rise of the "king of the North." We learned in chapter 10 that the king of the North is Russia and the federated Arab states. As nations go, communistic Russia is an upstart. At approximately the time of World War I, a revolution took place that delivered Russia into the hands of a small but dedicated group of individuals. From that small beginning Communism has become the ideology and power that dominates a great portion of the world's population today. This event has taken place within our lifetime, but the prophet Ezekiel outlined very clearly that Russia will gather together under her influence the Arab states. One of the questions in international relations today is "Whose side will the Near East take?"

Russia and Communism are dominating the thinking of the peoples of the Near East. According to Ezekiel 38, Russia will have designs on the land of Palestine. The power to the North will look to the riches of the unprotected state of Israel and will begin a great invasion.

If Russia were to move, one potential path would be south through the Caucasuses and into Palestine to join Egypt and swallow up the land of Israel. The rise of Russian influence among the Arab states is another significant factor that is one of the buds indicating that the coming of the Lord may be very near.

A third significant event is the rise of a coalition of nations of Europe under a common head. We studied the prophecies related to this in detail in Daniel 2, 7, and 8. We saw that the land of Palestine, throughout her long history, would be dominated by four great world empires—the Babylonians, the Medo-Persians, the Grecians, and the Romans. We also saw that the final form of the Roman Empire was represented by ten toes on the image and by ten horns on the Beast (Dan. 7). As we examined those Scriptures, we saw that a coalition of states, which had grown out of the old Roman Empire, would be brought together because of a common enemy, Russia.

The rise of Russia to a place of world power has brought fear to Europe. This fear, more than any other thing, is driving Europe toward the fulfillment of biblical prophecies. Since World War II European statesmen have continued to affirm that the only hope of maintaining peace and the balance of power is to bring the states of Europe under a common head to protect them from Communism.

The European Common Market seems like a very minor thing, but it is filled with significance. Nations that have had trade barriers for generations, and some for centuries, have broken these barriers because of their need to unite and thereby allow a free exchange and flow of goods throughout Europe and Great Britain. Although the Word of God says nothing specifically about the "common market," it fits the description of world powers at the end time.

Another step is that political leaders have conferred officially and unofficially to bring about some political alliance to supersede the common market. Two possibilities have been suggested. One is that the nations of Europe elect representatives to a common assembly, which would have authority over all of the federated states in that alliance. The second is that each nation of Europe in this alliance will maintain its sovereignty, but there will be a federation of independent governments. Most leaders seem to favor the union of the states of Europe in an alliance without establishing one governing or controlling body.

When we turn to the prophecies of Daniel 2 and 7, to Revelation 13 and 17, and to other parallel passages, we find that the final form of Gentile world power will be a federation of independent states that elect one person to take authority over them while they maintain their own sovereign authority. The Common Market in Europe and the movement toward a federation of nations indicates an imminent coming of our Lord. This is another bud on the stem.

The conditions in the visible church are another indication that we are living in the latter days of the church's stay on earth. "Now the Spirit speaketh expressly, that in the latter times some shall depart from the faith, giving heed to seducing spirits, and the doctrines of devils" (1 Tim. 4:1). Peter writes, "There were false prophets also among the people, even as there shall be false teachers among you, who privily shall bring in damnable heresies, even denying the Lord that bought them and bring upon themselves swift destruction. And many shall follow their pernicious ways; by reason of whom the way of truth shall be evil spoken of" (2 Pet. 2:1–2). This refers to repudiation of the revealed truth of the Word of God.

The picture of the final form of the visible church is given to us in Revelation 3, where the apostle John was preaching to the church at Laodicea: "I know thy works, that thou art neither cold not hot; I would thou wert cold or hot. So then because thou art lukewarm, and neither cold nor hot, I will spue thee out of my mouth" (v. 15). Then he addressed himself to those who call themselves a true church but who are false: "Behold, I stand at the door, and knock; if any man hear my voice, and open the door, I will come in to him, and will sup with him, and he with me" (v. 20). This church professes to be the church of the living God, the bride of Jesus Christ, but Christ is on the outside having to seek admission. His grace is manifested in that He is still willing to come in if His knock is heeded. "To him that overcometh will I grant to sit with me in my throne, even as I also overcame, and am set down with my Father in his throne" (v. 21).

In these passages we see a picture of a church that professes to know Christ but has left Him standing outside as if He were a stranger. Many of the great religious movements in our country that were once true to the Word of God have repudiated the authority of Scripture and are teaching that which is contrary to the Word of God. Organizations, institutions, and even denominations that formerly held to the truth of the Word of God have openly repudiated that faith. I believe this is one of the significant signs of the day in which we live.

If I picked out one future event here and one there, I might be accused of twisting something to make it *look* as though there were a possibility of a fulfillment of the Word of God. Then my message might be suspect. But when we consider the great movements of the tribulation and see that God could move in just a few moments of time to make the necessary things happen, the conclusion seems inescapable: the coming of the Lord MUST be drawing near. It is my absolute conviction that there is not one single line of prophecy that yet must be fulfilled before we can say, "He can come now."

If this interpretation is true, and if the coming of the Lord is very near, what should be our attitude? Matthew 24 has something to say about this. "As the days of Noah were, so shall also the coming of the Son of Man be. For as in the days that were before the flood they were eating and drinking, marrying and giving in marriage, until the day that Noah entered into the ark, and knew not until the flood came, and took them away, so shall also the coming of the Son of Man be" (vv. 37–39). I have heard preachers use these verses to prove that the number of marriages and divorces and the amount of liquor consumed in the United States has something to do with the return of the Lord. That simply wasn't what Christ was talking about. There is nothing wrong with eating and drinking or with marrying and giving in marriage. God made all of them a part of our lives.

The comparison between the days of Noah and those of the end time, I believe, has to do with God's warning of judgment. For a hundred years Noah warned people of coming judgment. He preached that God was going to send a catastrophe that would wipe out all unbelievers. He declared the grace and mercy of God and invited people to accept salvation and avoid judgment. Noah preached the longest sermon in history, a one-hundred-year sermon, but the only converts he had were his own family. The rest, occupied with routine activities, were indifferent to the warning.

Concerning the tribulation, Christ was saying that all the signs—the coming of the Federated States of Europe, the rise of Russia, the return of Israel to Palestine—would go unheeded. When the Lord Jesus Christ comes back to earth, there will be multitudes whose hearts were never stirred, whose consciences were never pricked, and who rejected the Gospel preached by believing witnesses during the tribulation. They were so occupied with the usual things that they missed the warning and the signs of judgment.

I believe the Lord says the same thing to us today. We become so engrossed in the normal activities of life— eating and drinking, marrying and giving in marriage, home, family, jobs, pleasures, vacations—that when we see the shadows cast by these momentous events we remain ignorant of their significance. God would say, "When you see the little green shoot, you know that a process has been started that will end in the harvest."

17

What Will We Do in Heaven?

Revelation 21:4

MOST BELIEVERS HAVE a nebulous concept of heaven. None of us has been there. People don't vacation there and return with slides to show their friends. Much of our concept of heaven has been fashioned by hymn writers or cartoonists. The hymn writers portray heaven as a place where believers sit in the shade with soft breezes keeping them cool as they relax day after day. The prospect seems monotonous. The cartoonist pictures the saints sitting on the edge of a cloud with their feet hanging over into nothingness, about to slip off into space. Floating on a cloud might be exciting to do once, but the activity would be of little interest after the novelty wore off.

The Bible says little about heaven. If God fully revealed to us its splendors and glories, we would never again be satisfied to live out our appointed years here. If we don't know much about what heaven looks like, or much about the surroundings or circumstances, the Bible has even less to say about what we will do for eternity. Yet, some hints are given. And these glimpses will create a desire to be absent from the body and present with the Lord, to be home in glory with Him.

Worshiping

When we see our Lord face to face, when we are brought into His presence in our redeemed, glorified bodies, we will be occupied in worship. John wrote, "And I heard a great voice out of heaven saying, 'Behold, the tabernacle of God is with men, and he will dwell with them, and they shall be his people, and God himself shall be with them, and be their God'" (Rev. 21:3).

John was thinking back to an Old Testament truth. God had appointed a meeting place between Himself and the nation Israel in the tabernacle. The plan of the tabernacle was revealed to Moses, and all of the sacrifices and worship carried on in the tabernacle were a matter of divine revelation. When God revealed the plan of the tabernacle to Moses, He said, "There will I meet with you."

The tabernacle was designed to be a meeting place between God and His people. There they could approach God through blood sacrifice. That is why prominence was given to the altar and the sacrifices that would be offered on it. Only those who had been cleansed could come into the presence of God. Those who come to God are to come with their offerings, prayers, and worship. The altar of incense was a revelation concerning worship. Those who come to God are to feed upon the Word of God; hence the table of shewbread. Those who had been

redeemed by blood and cleansed by the washing of the
water with the Word are to be lights to the world; hence
the lampstand.

Everything in the tabernacle looked toward the presence of God, revealed through the shining light above the
mercy seat on the ark in the holy of holies. Everything in
the tabernacle was designed to bring sinners into the presence of God as redeemed worshipers. "There will I meet
with you."

Turning from the past to the future, John said that the
tabernacle was only a foreshadowing of how God would
dwell with His people in the future and how they would
have access to God. And in eternity we will realize the
significance of the tabernacle—our access to God—and
we will become a worshiping people. God said, "Whoso
offereth praise glorifieth me" (Ps. 50:23).

Hebrews 13 says that even in the new age there are
certain sacrifices that God desires. The bloody sacrifices of
lambs, goats, and bullocks are no longer necessary because
the sacrifice of Christ was sufficient. Now God desires
sacrifices of worship and praise, even the fruit of our lips,
giving thanks to His name. Those who worship God recognize the splendor and the perfection of the character of
God, and those who offer thanksgiving recognize the gifts
that God has given to us.

Throughout eternity believers will be occupied primarily with giving worship, praise, and thanksgiving to
God because of who He is, because of His sovereign position over all creation. Things in heaven, in earth, and
under the earth shall bow before Him and give honor and
glory to Him. It will be the delight of God's children,
collectively and individually, to dwell with Him and to

worship Him. We are a worshiping people because of who God is, because of what He has done.

In the Old Testament there was a barrier between the worshiper and God: the veil. Only the high priest could go behind the veil, and even he could not go in without a blood offering. In the New Testament Christ became the veil. To get to God we must go through Him.

In the eternal state every veil will be taken away because the barrier of sin will be completely and perfectly removed. We will go into the presence of God and dwell with Him. We will be His people. God Himself will be with us and be our God. And we will worship Him.

Learning

In the eternal state we will also be students. Paul wrote, "When I was a child, I spake as a child, I understood as a child, I thought as a child: but when I became a man, I put away childish things. For now we see through a glass, darkly; but then face to face: now I know in part; but then shall I know even as also I am known" (1 Cor. 13:11–12).

Eternity will be spent not only in worshiping God but also in pursuing the knowledge of God. The Old Testament was God's revelation, and what people in that day knew of God they knew through that revelation. David, who walked with God and who communed with Him upon his bed at night, learned what he knew about God by searching the Scriptures, God's revelation to man. That is why David could say that they were his meat night and day.

When Jesus Christ came, He came to add revelation concerning God, not to do away with the Old Testament Scriptures. In John 10 Christ made it very clear that no man knows God except through the Son, who came from the bosom of the Father and who has revealed the Father. What we know of God today we know through the Scriptures and through the Son. But God cannot be contained in the pages of a book. John referred to that when he said that all the libraries of the world could not contain the volumes that could be written about God.

Jesus Christ did not fully reveal God. No one could comprehend complete revelation. Yet it is God's nature to reveal Himself; He takes no delight in hiding Himself or in being unknown. Because we have finite minds we can comprehend little of an infinite God. When we get to glory, when the limitations imposed by sin have all been taken away, God will reveal Himself. A finite God could reveal Himself totally and completely in a limited amount of time, but an infinite God may require all eternity to reveal Himself. In eternity we will be students. We will receive new revelation as an infinite God adds to what He has already disclosed so that we might know Him.

The great consuming passion of the apostle Paul was "That I may know him" (Phil. 3:10). The epistles convince us that Paul knew more about Jesus Christ and God than any other person. All Bible students and theologians since Paul's day have been trying to understand what Paul knew, but no one adds anything to the revelation already disclosed. But even with all that had been revealed to Paul he still knew only an infinitesimal part of what is to be known about God. But we will receive expanded knowledge when God reveals Himself and gives to His glorified saints the capacity to understand Him.

We are not infinite now and never will be. Therefore, God can never reveal Himself all at once to us. Little by little God will add to our understanding of Himself. I think that is what Paul had in mind when he said, "For now we see through a glass dimly; but then face to face."

John wrote, "And God shall wipe away all tears from their eyes; and there shall be no more death, neither sorrow, nor crying, neither shall there be any more pain: for the former things are passed away" (Rev. 21:4).

Throughout eternity we will receive not only a knowledge of God but a knowledge of how He deals with us. Many things happen every day that we simply do not understand and cannot explain; but God will not leave those riddles unsolved. He will wipe away tears from our eyes by explaining the mystery of His will. He will show us how He worked and why He permitted us to go through certain experiences.

Recently I received a call from a brokenhearted father who had been attending our services with his wife and children for some time. His seven-year-old son had been killed by a hit-and-run driver, and the father asked if I would conduct the funeral service. When I visited their home to talk and pray with them the mother said, "We can't understand it, and we know you can't explain it; but we believe that God makes no mistakes. Someday we'll understand." Those heartbroken parents would like to know why, and someday they will know, because a part of eternity, I believe, will be spent listening to God explain why things happened and how things worked together for good.

The sorrows, heartaches, and burdens we bear all will be lifted, and that will be a part of our learning process. Eternity will be spent receiving revelation concerning God and the mystery of His dealings, the wonder of His will.

What a joy to have this unfold. If we speak of eternity in terms of days and years, every day will bring a new revelation of the glory, splendor, and majesty of God.

Knowledge begets love, so the more we know of Him, the more we will love Him. He reveals Himself not simply to satisfy our intellectual curiosity, but to explain His working so that our love for Him will increase through the unending ages of eternity.

Fellowshiping

In describing the millennial age and Christ's relationship to millennial saints, John wrote, "They shall see his face" (Rev. 22:4). This suggests the idea of a personal, intimate fellowship between the child of God and the Lord Jesus Christ. Fellowship is the response of the mind, heart, and will of the child of God to the mind, heart, and will of Christ. It will be our privilege to enter into the fullness of fellowship. We will give our redeemed minds to the truth of God, our purified hearts to the love of Christ, and our wills to obey Him perfectly and implicitly through the unending ages of eternity.

When Jesus chose the disciples, He chose them "that they should be with him" (Mark 3:14). His primary purpose in selecting the Twelve was to provide fellowship for Himself and so that they would respond to His fellowship. The privilege of fellowship that the disciples enjoyed will be the privilege of every child of God. "We shall see His face."

When we are at home with the Lord, there will be no obstacles or barriers; there will be only personal, open communion between the Son of God and the child of God. It will be our delight to go into His presence and to experience what Mary did as she sat at His feet and heard His words. She communed with Him.

We will be occupied not only in fellowship with Christ but also in fellowship with other believers. Paul said, "Then shall I know even as also I am known" (1 Cor. 13:12). This referred to fellowship between a believer and other believers as well as to fellowship between the believer and Christ.

One of the joys of being a pastor is meeting those who want to become a part of the fellowship of the church. When people come before our board we always ask them how they came to know Jesus Christ as Savior. Every testimony is different, but each is a miracle of God's grace. I will not be satisfied until I hear all the saints recite how they came to know Christ as Savior. It will be thrilling to hear the saints recount the marvel of God's grace.

Fellowship depends on knowledge. The reason we don't have real fellowship today is because we don't know each other. We never seem to have time enough to get to know each other here, but there we will. We don't know Abraham, David, Elijah, Zechariah, Peter, or Paul. But someday we will. We will spend time with them, lots of it. Together we will recount the goodness of God's grace and get to know one another as members of the family of God.

Working

"His servants shall serve him" (Rev. 22:3). We live in bodies that grow weak, get tired, and need food. When the Bible says "there remaineth therefore a rest to the people of God," we think it means a cessation of all activity. Rest is not cessation of activity, but a change of activity.

During summer vacation somebody asked me, "Are you having a good rest this summer?"

"I certainly am," I replied.

"What have you been doing?"

"I'm painting my house," I answered.

"You call that rest?"

Yes, to me that is rest. Several years ago we took one of the fellows from the church up to a lake cottage with us. We told him we were going up for a rest. We did what we usually do when we rest: we cut trees, sawed them up for firewood, cleared brush, and mowed the lawn. He said at the end of the day, "You call this rest?" Yes, to me that was rest, but he went home exhausted.

When we speak of heaven as a place of rest, it is not a place where nothing is done. Scripture says His servants shall serve Him. God will have some work for every one of His children to do that will occupy them through eternity. I don't know the nature of the work, but I know we will work.

Work was not a curse. It was a blessing given by God to Adam in the garden before the fall. Before Adam sinned he was told that he was to cultivate the garden. The curse added perspiration to work, but work itself was not the curse. For eternity we will be working, and we will be occupied for Him.

The word translated "serve" here is the same word that is used of the service of a priest in the temple. It shows that no matter what work God assigns us to do, God will view it as a priestly ministry. It will be the worship and service that are rendered unto God by those who have been set apart to God. Each child of God will contribute something to the welfare of the body of the redeemed.

What one does, no other person could possibly do, and we will all depend on each other.

We will spend eternity worshiping, learning, fellowshiping, and working. All these center on a person: Christ. We worship Him, learn of Him, fellowship with Him, and serve Him. God gives us a foretaste of heaven now. We can worship now, learn of Him now, fellowship with Him now, and serve now. That is why the hymn writer said,

> Blessed assurance,
> Jesus is mine.
> Oh, what a foretaste of glory divine.

18

What Will Heaven Be Like?

Revelation 21–22

THE APOSTLE JOHN gave a glimpse of what heaven will be like in Revelation 21–22. It is impossible to fully comprehend a realm we have never seen, and it is difficult to translate heaven into earthly terms we can understand. The glory of God's presence is so far beyond human comprehension that John described it in terms of reflected sunlight, gleaming gems, and glittering gold that has been polished to mirror brilliance.

Ezekiel faced the same problem. In the first chapter of his prophecy he recorded the glory of God that was revealed to him. The dazzling brilliance of the Shekinah of God burst upon him. He described it as the sun shining on polished jewels. The apostle John, speaking about the glory of the resurrected Christ in Revelation 1, compared it to sunlight shining upon new-fallen snow.

Heaven, first of all, is the presence of God. This does not mean that heaven is not a place, for it certainly is; but heaven is more than that. We should think of it, first of all, as the place of God's revealed presence, where He displays His glory. John wrote concerning the redeemed: "They shall see his face" (Rev. 22:4). Christ, intimating the same truth, said, "And if I go and prepare a place for you, I will come again, and receive you unto myself; that where I am, there ye may be also" (John 14:3). The apostle Paul, in 1 Thessalonians 4:16–17, said that the Lord Himself shall descend from heaven with a voice of the archangel, with a shout and with the trump of God, and the living shall be caught up together with the resurrected in the clouds to meet the Lord in the air and so shall we ever be with the Lord.

The Bible never says Christ will come to take us to heaven. It says He will come to take us to Himself, to take us home to the Father, to take us into the Father's house. To be "in heaven" is to be in the presence of God the Father, God the Son, and God the Holy Spirit. When we realize that this is the Scriptural concept of heaven it makes the question so often asked, "Where is heaven?" of little importance. Do not try to fix heaven in a place. Heaven is the presence of God.

When Christ was in conflict with the Pharisees they tried to discredit Him with a question for which they believed there was no answer. According to the Pharisees, a man had died, leaving his wife a widow. The man's brother married his widowed sister-in-law, as required by Levitical law, but then he too died. So the next brother married her, but he also died. Eventually all seven brothers married her and died. The trick question the Pharisees asked Jesus was, "In the resurrection, which one of the brothers will claim her as his wife?" The Lord answered,

"The children of this world marry, and are given in marriage: but they which shall be accounted worthy to obtain that world, and the resurrection from the dead, neither marry, nor are given in marriage: Neither can they die any more: for they are equal [or they are like] unto the angels; and are the children of God, being the children of the resurrection" (Luke 20:34–36).

We know that angels dwell in the presence of God and are dispatched from His presence according to His will to fulfill His commands. In resurrection, Christ said, the redeemed will be like angels. He was not speaking primarily of their physical appearance. He was speaking of their residence.

Paul said in 1 Corinthians 15 that there are different kinds of bodies. On this earth there are bodies of birds, fishes, and people. Paul also said that there are bodies suited to existence on earth and bodies suited to existence in heaven. Angels are not disembodied spirits floating around like a wisp of cloud. Angels dwell in celestial bodies suited for heaven, and in these celestial bodies they are in the presence of God. According to Christ's teaching in Luke 20:36 the resurrected will be like angels in that they will dwell in celestial bodies in the presence of God.

To reveal something about heaven and about life in the presence of God, Revelation 21–22 emphasizes the description of a city. In Revelation 21:10 John said that he was carried in the spirit to a great and high mountain and was showed that great city, the holy Jerusalem, descending out of heaven from God. John intended to convey a number of details about heaven by referring to it as a city.

The first city mentioned in the Word of God was founded by Nimrod (Gen. 10), and its history is given in

Genesis 11. Before that time people apparently did not live in cities but they joined together in Babel to organize their rebellion against God, to unite in their opposition to God and in their repudiation of His truth; all who lived there were apostates and renegades. To declare themselves independent of God they united in their unbelief, knowing they could not continue their rebellion as independent, isolated individuals.

"But ye are come unto mount Zion, and unto the city of the living God, the heavenly Jerusalem" (Heb. 12:22). The emphasis here is on the city again. In this heavenly Jerusalem several groups are identifiable. First, he mentioned "an innumerable company of angels" (v. 22). This referred to all the unfallen angels who have faithfully served God from the time of their creation, having resisted the temptation of Lucifer, who sought to draw all the angels after himself. This heavenly city will be occupied by unfallen angels.

Second, he mentioned the "general assembly and church of the first born" (v. 23). I believe this refers to the church of this age, the church that is Christ's body, which began at Pentecost and will continue until the rapture. The second identifiable group of inhabitants is the church of this present age.

The third group is "the spirits of just men made perfect" (v. 23). Evidently this refers to all Old Testament saints from the time of Adam to the inception of the church, and to tribulation saints from the rapture to the second advent. It also includes all millennial saints, those born and redeemed in the millennial age. This is a third, separate, identifiable group.

The church and the spirits of just men—the Old Testament saints and the New Testament saints—comprise the total body of the redeemed. They are all there by faith through grace, based on the death of Christ; but they are there in a different relationship to Christ. The church is there as His bride. The Old Testament saints are there as friends of the Bridegroom. They are related to Christ. They are within the body of the redeemed. God, the Judge of all, is in the city (Heb. 12:23) and "Jesus the mediator of the new covenant" (v. 24) will also be there. Thus, along with the unfallen angels, the Old Testament saints, and the church saints, the Father and the Son are present. The redeemed who occupy this heavenly city are together in the presence of God.

John described this city in Revelation 21. He said it has the "glory of God" (v. 11). John saw this city descending from heaven the same way the pillar of fire or the cloud descended from heaven and hovered over the tabernacle in the Old Testament. As it descended from heaven it displayed the glory of God. The city was glorious and its light was like a precious stone, even like a jasper stone, clear as crystal (v. 11). Jasper is a diamond or a colorless stone. When polished it radiates and reflects light with dazzling brilliance. To describe the city's glory, John said it was like the light of the sun reflected in a diamond. The city is not glorious because of what it is made of but because God is personally present.

David collected gold, silver, timber, and stones to build a temple in Jerusalem. Solomon constructed the temple, and when it was dedicated the Shekinah glory of God filled it. The glory of the temple was not its gold and silver. Its glory was God's presence. The tabernacle in the wilderness was made of linen and animal skins, and after a time in the desert it probably was drab and dull, uninteresting to the sight; but when God moved into that tabernacle and filled it, then it was glorious—not because of the cunning work in the materials nor because of the skins that had been dyed—but because God was personally present.

In Revelation 21 John said that this city is the home of all the redeemed, together with the unfallen angels who are in God's presence. The redeemed behold God's glory and, like diamonds, radiate and reflect it. John was not emphasizing the place nor the materials; he was emphasizing a relationship to a Person.

This city is a protected place; it has a high wall with twelve gates (21:12). The ancient city walls were erected for the inhabitants' protection. They had walls high enough to prevent any adversary from scaling them and gates strong enough to keep any adversary from battering them down. A city was as safe as its gates and walls. In describing the place where we will dwell, John emphasized that it is a protected city, where the inhabitants will live in perfect safety and security, without fear. Although this city has gates they shall not "be shut at all by day: for there shall be no night there" (v. 25). What is the purpose of having gates if they are always open? The residents do not dwell in safety because of the physical gates; they are safe because of the One in whose presence they dwell. The emblems of security are there, but the inhabitants do not depend on them for security. They depend on the One in whose presence they rest.

So heaven will be a place of rest, safety, and security because the redeemed are in God's presence, and God's holiness sets bounds so that no unholy thing can approach. Were it possible for someone to climb out of hell, he still could not enter God's presence to corrupt the city nor the saints because the holiness of God protects residents from every danger.

The city will have twelve foundations (v. 14). The foundations relate to the permanence of the city. When builders prepare to build, they dig down to solid rock to place the foundations, because when a building is founded upon rock, it is unshakable and unmovable. The building's permanence depends on the foundation upon which it rests. This city is permanent because it has foundations. In the foundation are the names of the twelve apostles of the Lamb. Our Lord said to Peter, "Thou art Peter, and upon this rock [Myself] I will build my church" (Matt. 16:18). Christ is the foundation. Paul told the Corinthians that "other foundation can no man lay than that which is laid, which is Christ Jesus" (1 Cor. 3:11). This city is founded upon the eternal rock, the Son of God, and He is its foundation.

The city will be spacious, built on a square, and the length is as large as the breadth. The measure of the city was 12,000 furlongs, which is approximately 1,500 miles. Some visualize this as a cube with four dimensions. Others view it as a pyramid with three dimensions. Whatever shape it is, it is spacious. Today 1,500 miles is not far, but it was in John's day. Christ was born in Nazareth, thirty miles inland from the Mediterranean Sea, but Scripture doesn't record that He ever saw the sea. He traveled the ninety miles from Galilee to Jerusalem because He was compelled to attend the feasts. When John spoke of a city 1,500 miles by 1,500 miles by 1,500 miles, he was speaking of that which was beyond comprehension. John was trying to communicate the spaciousness of the city, not necessarily its physical dimensions. The city will be big enough to bring all of the redeemed ones of God into the Father's presence.

The twelve precious stones that adorn the city emphasize the city's beauty. The beauty is not in streets of gold, gates of pearls, nor walls decked with jewels. He used these to convey indescribable beauty. The beauty of God is His holiness. This city will reveal and reflect the beauty of holiness, and those who dwell in the city as holy ones will display and reflect the glory of God, the glory of His holiness. God's glory will fill every part of the city.

When Zechariah closed his prophecy concerning Christ's earthly reign, he said that all the pots, vessels, and houses shall be holiness to the Lord, and even the bells of the horses' harnesses will sound out holiness to the Lord. He was showing us that God's character will permeate everything. Ordinary things will reflect the beauty of God's holiness just as the tabernacle and the temple in the Old Testament reflected the glory of God.

"And the city had no need of the sun, neither of the moon, to shine in it: for the glory of God did lighten it, and the Lamb is the light thereof" (Rev. 21:23). In this city there is no darkness. God sent darkness to provide for our physical rejuvenation through sleep. But we invented floodlights so we can do what God never intended us to do—work through the night. We need the rest of the night. But in that city there will be no need for night because there will be no weakness, no loss of strength. We won't need rest because our bodies will not become tired and exhausted. The one who came as light into the world will cause His light to shine throughout the city so that we will walk in the light of His countenance. Children are never afraid of the sunshine, only of the dark. They're not afraid of what is revealed in the daylight; they're afraid of what lurks in the shadows. When John said there would be no night there, he was reminding us that God has removed every cause of fear, and He brings peace by His presence. The city will be a fearless place.

"In the midst of the street of it, and on either side of the river, was there the tree of life, which bare twelve manner of fruits, and yielded her fruit every month: and the leaves of the tree were for the healing of the nations" (22:2). To understand the picture given here, think of the city as a pyramid rather than as a square. Beginning at the top of the pyramid is a street that goes round and round until it reaches the bottom. Alongside that street is an aqueduct that carries water from the throne of God at the apex of the pyramid. The water that proceeds "out of the throne of God" (22:1) flows along that street. Along that watercourse grows a tree that bears fruit every month. Fruit is good for just one purpose—to be consumed. The first thing God gave Adam after giving him Eve was fruit to eat. John added that the leaves of the tree were for healing or for sustaining the nations. In the Garden of Eden people could eat, but they didn't have to eat to stay alive. Before Adam fell, there was no corruption or death in his body. God told Adam he could eat the fruit of every tree except one. This seems to have been for Adam's enjoyment—not to keep body and soul together—but to provide a basis of fellowship. After all, when we want to fellowship with someone, we frequently eat together. God will provide a basis for fellowship together.

This fruit does something else. It reminds us that God is our constant source of provision. God enables us to eat and provides the fruit, so in eating we commemorate that

He is our manna, our living bread, and that He will sustain us throughout eternity.

In his description of this city John was emphasizing that cities, although they were started by people in rebellion against God, will end with people in subjection to God.

People are gregarious by nature. Every individual has a need for someone else. God recognized that in Adam. That's why He gave Eve to Adam. We need each other, and it is sin that has driven us apart. When we are at home with the Father we will enjoy living as neighbors. We will be brought into the Father's presence. We will be at home with Him and in the company of all the redeemed of all the ages. We will behold God's glory and be protected and preserved by Him.

"Eye hath not seen, nor ear heard, neither have entered into the heart of man, the things which God hath prepared for them that love him" (1 Cor. 2:9). Heaven will be a permanent home of indescribable beauty because it is filled with God's presence. It will be a place of safety and security, where we will dwell without fear and where for eternity we will be sustained by God's provision.

Note to the Reader

The publisher invites you to share your response to the message of this book by writing Discovery House Publishers, Box 3566, Grand Rapids, MI 49501, USA. For information about other Discovery House books, music, or videos, contact us at the same address or call 1-800-653-8333. Find us on the Internet at http://www.dhp.org/ or send E-mail to books@dhp.org.

Other Discovery House books that will feed your soul with the Word of God:

Designed To Be Like Him
by *J. Dwight Pentecost*
    This new edition of a classic study offers a thoughtful analysis of the teaching of the whole New Testament on Christian living.

A Faith That Endures
by *J. Dwight Pentecost*
    A faithful guide through the rich historical meaning and the many contemporary applications of the book of Hebrews.

The Joy Of Intimacy With God
by *J. Dwight Pentecost*
    This Bible study guide to the truths of 1 John is designed to explore and enable you to enjoy a life of fellowship with God.

Broken Things: Why We Suffer
by *M. R. De Haan, M. D.*
    To those seeking reasons for their suffering and disappointments, this book offers hope and peace through the healing principles of God's Word.

What Jesus Said About Successful Living
by *Haddon W. Robinson*
    Through a careful, fascinating study of Matthew 5, 6 and 7, the author shows what Christ taught in the Sermon on the Mount.

Daniel: God's Man in a Secular Society
by *Donald K. Campbell*

Intriguing, contemporary perspective and helpful application of the prophecies in Daniel. A call to radical dependence on God.

Our Daily Times With God: *Favorite selections from Our Daily Bread*

A powerful devotional book featuring the best from *Our Daily Bread*, organized by themes and the great events of Scripture. Also available in a Large Print edition.

My Utmost for His Highest
by *Oswald Chambers*

The classic devotional bestseller. These powerful words will refresh those who need encouragement, brighten the way of those in difficulty, and strengthen personal relationships with Christ. A book to use every day for the rest of your life.

Order from your favorite bookstore or from:

DISCOVERY HOUSE PUBLISHERS
Box 3566
Grand Rapids, MI 49501
Call toll-free: 1-800-653-8333